Endorsements for

THE MIRROR

"Koulopoulos goes well beyond traditional thinking about the power and impact of AI. He asks the fundamental question of whether AI is no longer just 'artificial,' and if not, how far it can take us in understanding the depth and use of our own intelligence. Tom brings a new perspective to what's ahead."

—**James Champy**, *New York Times* bestselling author, *Reengineering the Corporation*

"Koulopoulos forces us to look at AI through an entirely different lens—beyond tech hype and fear and toward how intelligent machines will challenge us to redefine meaning, leadership, and what it means to be human. Koulopoulos doesn't talk about AI. He forces us to consider what AI reveals about us."

—**Greg Dracon**, partner, .406 Ventures

"In *The Mirror*, Koulopoulos challenges us to see AI not as the end of human relevance, but as the beginning of a new era. AI will surely reshape the future of work. In healthcare our future will be determined not only by how we leverage evolving technology, but by how we do so with purpose, wisdom, and an authentic focus on the art of healing."

—**Michael Dandorph**, president and CEO, Tufts Medicine

"*The Mirror* reframes AI not as a tool, but as a test of human judgment. As intelligence becomes abundant, responsibility intensifies. Koulopoulos makes clear that human oversight, accountability, and moral authority must remain firmly in control. Essential reading for leaders who understand that the future of AI will be defined not by what machines can do, but by what humans choose to allow."

—**Barry P. Chaiken**, MD, bestselling author, *Navigating the Code*

"*The Mirror* doesn't just explain AI's future, it challenges us to decide what kind of future we want."

—**Venkat Venkatraman**, professor emeritus, Boston University, co-author of *Fusion Strategy*

"In *The Mirror,* Thomas Koulopoulos elevates the AI conversation from capability to consequence, challenging leaders to focus not on what machines can do, but on what humans must stand for. As intelligence becomes abundant, he makes a compelling case that sustained leadership advantage will be defined by meaning, judgment, and human insight—core to how we lead and perform in the Intelligent Age. A timely and thought-provoking guide for leaders committed to shaping a future grounded in purpose, stewardship, and human flourishing."

—**Rory Hendrikz**, VP, Hult Ashridge Executive Education

"An excellent look at how AI will take humans to new levels of capability. *The Mirror* reimagines AI not just as a tool for productivity, but as a means to enhance human cognitive and imaginative abilities. Rather than replacing people, AI empowers them to move beyond speed and optimization toward deeper judgment, synthesis, and ethical awareness, marking a shift from the 'Knowledge Worker' to the 'Wisdom Worker'—where wisdom, creativity, and responsibility become the hallmarks of professional excellence."

—**Omar Ishrak**, former chairman & CEO, Medtronic

THE MIRROR

Also by Thomas Koulopoulos

Revealing the Invisible:
How Our Hidden Behaviors Are Becoming
the Most Valuable Commodity of the 21st Century

Reimagining Healthcare:
How the Smartsourcing Revolution Will Drive
the Future of Healthcare and Refocus It
on What Matters Most, the Patient

Gigatrends:
Six Forces That Are Changing
the Future for Billions

THE MIRROR

Finding Meaning and Purpose in the Age of Artificial Intelligence

THOMAS KOULOPOULOS

Post Hill
PRESS

A POST HILL PRESS BOOK

ISBN: 979-8-89565-804-8
ISBN (eBook): 979-8-89565-805-5

The Mirror:
Finding Meaning and Purpose in the Age of Artificial Intelligence

Cover design by Molly Seabrook
Interior design and composition by Greg Johnson, Textbook Perfect

The cover juxtaposes a classical image of Narcissus, symbolizing human self-reflection, with a digitally fragmented mirror below. This contrast visualizes the book's central premise: As we look into artificial intelligence, our reflection becomes refracted, altered, and reinterpreted. The mirror is no longer simply a reflection of who we are, but a transformation of how we understand ourselves.

Post Hill
PRESS

Post Hill Press
New York • Nashville
posthillpress.com

Published in the United States of America
1 2 3 4 5 6 7 8 9 10

Printed in Canada

For Mia and Adam,
May you always have the wisdom to see yourselves clearly,
and the courage to become more than you see.

Contents

Foreword

In the AI era, the speed at which you think is the speed at which you win. Not the speed of your infrastructure. Not the speed of your deployment pipeline. The speed of your thinking—your willingness to act on what's possible, not just what's proven. Here is the discipline that separates those who will lead from those who will follow: whatever limitations or impediments you face with today's technology, you must plan and act as if they will be solved in the next few weeks or months. Because they will be. The window between "this is impossible" and "this is table stakes" has collapsed from years to months. If you wait for certainty, you will be perpetually late. The leaders of this moment are not the ones who waited for the technology to be ready. They are the ones who were already thinking at the speed the technology was racing toward.

Two questions will define this decade. Can we harness the full potential of AI? And can we build AI that can actually be trusted? Both have to be answered. Neither can wait.

Tom Koulopoulos gets this. *The Mirror* is not a book about what AI can do. It's a book about what AI demands of us—and the window we have to get it right.

Here's the shift most people are missing: AI agents aren't tools. Tools do what you tell them. Agents have a degree of autonomy, a level of opacity, and—if left without guardrails—an ambition of their own. That changes everything. When you bring a new team member into your organization, you interview them, check their references, assign them a manager, and give them increasing autonomy as trust is earned. We need to apply that same discipline to AI. The supply chain governance, the behavioral guardrails, the checks and balances—these aren't bureaucratic overhead. They're the price of trust.

What makes this urgent is that the window to shape AI is closing. Right now, humans still define how these systems are built and what values they carry. Within a few years, AI will be building AI. The exponential curve becomes vertical. At that point, the defaults we set today become the architecture of tomorrow—and we lose the ability to easily course-correct.

Tom's core argument is one I've arrived at independently: intelligence is being commoditized. It already is, it's just not evenly distributed yet. The question is what becomes rare and valuable when intelligence is abundant. His answer—wisdom, intentionality, the quality of the questions we ask—is exactly right. The people and organizations that thrive won't be the ones who know the most. They'll be the ones who direct intelligence toward the right ends, with judgment, ethics, and purpose.

That's why this book matters beyond the technology conversation. The real decisions here are societal. What do we preserve? What do we redesign? How do we make sure AI reaches everyone—not just those who can already afford it?

Those aren't questions for technologists alone. They're for all of us. And we don't have unlimited time to answer them.

Read this book. Then act like you mean it.

—***Jeetu Patel,***
President and Chief Product Officer, Cisco

Introduction

"We do not see things as they are, we see them as we are."

—ANAÏS NIN

For decades, we've been telling ourselves the same story about technology: that it's a tool that amplifies our ability to do work. Artificial intelligence changes that story in a way no technology has before.

AI is not just a tool. It's the first technology capable of acting autonomously to pursue human goals. For the first time, we have created something that not only extends our reach but also reveals our reasoning, biases, creativity, and contradictions—with disturbing clarity. It's a mirror. It exposes aspects of humanity that increasing complexity has allowed us to overlook.

AI is not just a tool. It's the first technology capable of acting autonomously to pursue human goals.

The real question isn't "What will AI do to *us*?" It's "What will *we* choose to become because of AI?" The answer to that question may seem far too challenging to imagine at this early stage of AI's development, but the goal of this book is to provide a glimpse into what that future might look like and to explore some of the existential questions that AI will inevitably ask of us. If intelligence is no longer our distinguishing advantage, we are forced to reconsider what gives human life its unique value and whether consciousness itself carries implications we have yet to fully understand.

By now, we've all heard that AI is an existential threat to humanity, that it will cause mass unemployment, and that a superintelligence will see us in the same light that we see species of lesser intelligence, as servants to our needs. While we will examine the need to scrutinize the evolution of AI, this book takes a different approach to understanding its impact by focusing on how AI will elevate humanity, illuminating the promise of a future in which AI helps us flourish as a species.

For five decades, I've watched and written about each generation of digital technology as it arrived with great fanfare and promise: mainframes, departmental computers, the personal computer, the internet, mobile devices, and cloud computing. Each one extended our capability, expanded our reach, and accelerated our productivity. But none of them challenged what it meant to be the ones doing the thinking.

AI is the first technology that not only extends what we can do, but also reveals how we think. Once you see this, it's impossible to ignore.

This book is not just about our fears. It is an unapologetically aspirational perspective on the long-term implications of AI. I've attempted to explore in a balanced and accurate way what it means to share the world with something more intelligent than us, and how that will cause us to reimagine our value, our work, our societies, and our sense of meaning and identity.

AI is the first external intelligence capable of illuminating the invisible patterns within us. As it begins to manage the mechanics of our lives, our organizations, and our society, the familiar structures of education, careers, politics, economies, expertise, and the standard metrics we have come to use as hallmarks of human progress and intelligence start to dissolve. In their place emerge structures and systems that are far more fluid: a landscape in which the value of humans and their institutions is no longer tied to deeply embedded notions of intelligence but to meaning.

I call this new epoch the *Intelligent Age.*

AI is the first external intelligence capable of illuminating the invisible patterns within us.

Throughout history, intelligence has been a scarce resource that we have sought to make more common through education. We are entering an era in which AI will make intelligence abundant, perhaps the single greatest resource on which we will build the future.

In the Intelligent Age, work will not disappear. Instead, we will redefine what makes human work valuable. AI will also become a force in global politics, used both as an asset and as a weapon. Nations that once competed for territory will now also compete for intelligence.

Clearly, we will face challenges as we experience these changes. However, the Intelligent Age also creates the possibility of the first genuinely global form of intelligence and a way for humanity to think together at a scale we have never achieved before. In that regard, AI will become a means of building bridges across cultural, economic, and social systems on a scale that could create a new era of global cooperation and interdependence.

All of this will change us in ways we can hardly begin to imagine. But the biggest change, and the main theme of this book, is the change that will happen within us. When intelligence is no longer rare and no longer our human advantage, we will have to

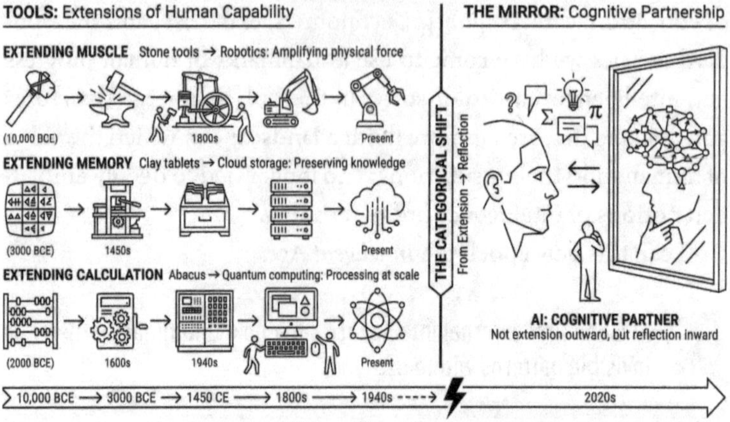

Figure I. From Tools to the Mirror: The Categorical Shift. The timelines show humanity's continuous extension of muscle (stone tools → robotics), memory (clay tablets → cloud storage), and calculation (abacus → quantum computing) are capabilities we still extend simultaneously. AI, which represents a radical departure, is not another tool and an extension outward, but a cognitive partner—the mirror—that reflects our thinking back to us, symbolizing the categorical shift from tool to cognitive partner.

develop a deeper understanding of the one thing machines cannot copy: human consciousness. AI will make us ask a question that has always been hard to answer: If machines can match or surpass our intelligence, memory, analysis, and even our creativity, *what does it mean to be conscious, and what unique value does that give us?*

AI creates conditions that make the question of what it means to be human unavoidable. For centuries, we've tied our worth to what we produce. Intelligence was a source of pride, and work gave us purpose. But AI breaks the assumption that these things define human worth. Instead, it exposes how old limits have constrained the full expression of human potential.

This book follows that journey, from the shock of new ideas, through changes in work and society, to the global challenges of trust and power, and finally to the personal growth the Intelligent Age asks of us.

If machines can match or surpass our intelligence, memory, analysis, and even our creativity, *what does it mean to be conscious, and what unique value does that give us?*

I have no doubt that some will find the future I am projecting idealistic, or even Pollyannish. But the same would have been thought during so many prior societal transformations that altered the world in ways once inconceivable.

In 1800, telling a farmer that his great-grandchildren would work in factories, live in cities of millions, and travel faster than a horse could run would have seemed an absurd fantasy, disconnected from the realities of life tied to the land and the seasons. In 1900, suggesting that within a lifetime, ordinary people would fly across oceans, communicate instantly across continents, and witness events happening on the other side of the world from their living rooms, would have strained credulity. In 1950, predicting that within decades, a teenager in rural India could access more information than existed in the Library of Alexandria, or that computers would fit in our pockets and mediate nearly every aspect of modern life, would have seemed like science fiction.

Each of these transformations was resisted, feared, and dismissed as unrealistic by those who could not imagine life beyond the constraints they knew. And yet each fundamentally redefined what it meant to be human, where we lived, how we worked, what we knew, and how we connected with one another.

Every so often, the world changes in ways so dramatic that it exceeds our capacity to envision the future. We are living through one of those moments. The Intelligent Age is not a minor adjustment to the past or an incremental departure from it. It's a civilizational shift as profound as the agricultural revolution that created permanent settlements, the industrial revolution that moved humanity from farms to factories, or the digital revolution that connected the planet. What seems idealistic today will seem inevitable tomorrow, not because the future is predetermined, but because once the tools exist, they reshape the very ground on which we stand.

In the end, the story of AI isn't about machines becoming more like humans. It's about humans being forced to confront what, beyond intelligence and productivity, actually defines us. This isn't about survival or scarcity, but about imagination, responsibility, conscience, compassion, and meaning.

I wrote this book to offer a ray of hope to anyone who feels that the stories we've relied on no longer fit the world we're entering. You don't need a technical background—just a sense that things are changing and a willingness to look honestly into the mirror that AI now holds up to us. Most of all, you need to do one thing: get comfortable with a question that does not yet have an obvious answer: Who will we choose to become when intelligence is no longer a limitation but a near-infinite resource for all?

What you'll find in the pages ahead isn't fear or hype. It's not a story about machines becoming more capable, but about how humanity responds when capability is no longer scarce. It's an invitation to reimagine a future that isn't waiting to be predicted. It's waiting to be created.

Who will we choose to become when intelligence is no longer a limitation but a near-infinite resource for all?

CHAPTER 1

When Technology Looks Back at Us

"The capability of human life is beyond our imagination. What counts is the human capacity to investigate and transform our own mind and the world around us."

—DALAI LAMA

Long before AI, some of the oldest philosophical traditions wrestled with a deceptively simple problem: Why is the self so difficult to see clearly? In the ancient Indian tradition of Advaita Vedānta,[1] one metaphor used to explain this is the mirror. What we experience as "me," it suggests, is not the self itself, but a reflection that's filtered through memory, habit, belief, fear, and desire. The mistake is not in seeing the reflection, but in assuming that what appears in the mirror is the source.

The fundamental shift, according to this way of thinking, doesn't come from sharper analysis or better reasoning. It comes from a quieter realization: that what you are observing is always one step removed, and that the act of seeing points beyond what is seen. The mirror can show you an image, but what is revealed is not the self, it's the lens through which the self is seen.

AI introduces a new version of this ancient problem that's externalized, accelerated, and technologized. For the first time, we have built a mirror that speaks back to us. It reflects our language, our patterns of thought, our values, our blind spots, our brilliance, and our bias in uncannily accurate ways. But reflection is not awareness.

We start mistaking the reflection for the source. AI doesn't matter because it's becoming human, but because it's forcing us to confront what being human really means. AI doesn't tell us who we are. It shows us what we project.

AI exposes the gap between the stories we tell about ourselves and the patterns we actually produce—a contrast many find unsettling. It's about the gap between who we believe we are and how we actually behave, collectively, when no one is watching. Except now, something always is.

For centuries, we were always the ones in control of our tools. AI is different. It shows us who we really are, without trying to agree or flatter us. It doesn't soften the truth or leave out the uncomfortable parts. And while it does so, it slowly takes over control of more and more of what we once considered uniquely human tasks.

AI doesn't matter because it's becoming human, but because it's forcing us to confront what being human really means.

That is the real disruption of the Intelligent Age: not just that machines will surpass us, but that they will reflect patterns without accommodation or reassurance. AI will inherit the many contradictions and flaws that make us human, without the accompanying human traits, such as empathy and morality.

AI turns introspection from a luxury into a responsibility. As it takes on more of the tedium that has defined so much of human work, it also frees us to rethink what our role and unique value will be.

A Detour on the Journey to Enlightenment

Thousands of years before the advent of computers, humanity expressed intelligence through an almost stubborn devotion to building things that mattered. Across the ancient world, from Petra to Athens, Ephesus to Cairo, human beings shaped stone with a precision and detail that still feels hard to explain.

The Treasury, the Parthenon, the pyramids, and the Library of Celsus didn't come from better tools. They came from people who had enough breathing room to think past their next meal or the next season. They shared a sense that there was more to build than what was strictly necessary. It's impossible to walk the ancient mosaic-lined streets of Ephesus and not feel that this was a civilization that had achieved a level of enlightenment that rivals our own.

Their efforts are a testament to the fact that when the need to provide for survival lessens, humanity doesn't settle into comfort. Instead, we become uneasy in a different way. Curiosity creeps in, leading us to take on projects that may not have an obvious or immediate payoff. Our attention begins looking inward, toward questions of meaning and spirituality, questions that reveal more of our humanity.

You see this happen again and again if you look closely at history. When physical work is augmented or replaced by machines, be they the levers that moved stone blocks to build pyramids or looms to weave textiles, people don't stop putting in effort. Work doesn't disappear. It shifts. Inevitably, we find entirely new ways to create value and find meaning.

Meaning doesn't arrive because life has become comfortable. It arrives because life finally loosens enough to leave room for us to think.

We have created monuments, temples, and art because we finally had time to ask why life mattered and to think beyond the constraints of our past.

Clearly, these past eras didn't free society from manual labor, but they gave rise to a class of workers whose purpose was to make meaning. The value of work was beyond functional; it was meaningful.

However, that same evolution from survival to enlightenment also led to societies becoming more complex. The drudgery of human toil didn't disappear; it simply shifted. For many, the physical grind lessened as the cognitive grind increased.

During the last two hundred years, we've dramatically expanded access to knowledge and literacy. Information is available at unprecedented speed with the advent of the internet. By nearly every measure, societies are far more educated. But hidden in this apparent democratization of knowledge is a fundamental structural paradox.

Consider that since 1800, human population has skyrocketed from one billion to over eight billion, which represents an eightfold increase in just over two centuries. Education systems raced to keep pace with that population explosion. Average schooling worldwide jumped from barely three years in 1950 to nearly eight years by 2010. It was a massive win for global literacy and mass education.

On the surface, it looked like we'd successfully swapped an economy built on brawn to one built on brainpower. But there was a serious flaw in that transformation. Educating the masses required that schools use the same mechanics as factory-floor logic, prioritizing throughput and standardization.

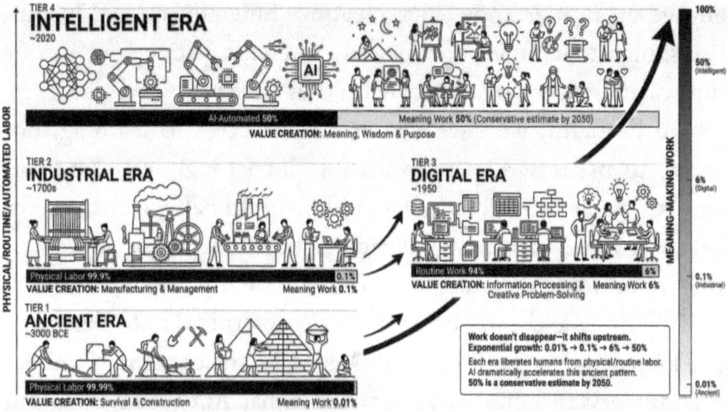

Figure 1.1. The Upstream Shift: Exponential Growth Toward Meaning Work. Across four eras—Ancient (3000 BCE), Industrial (1700s), Digital (1950), and Intelligent (2020)—human work has shifted from physical labor toward meaning-making through exponential growth: 0.01 percent → 0.1 percent → 6 percent → 50 percent. The ascending tiers and bold diagonal arrow visualize this upstream progression, with the curve steepening dramatically in the Intelligent Age. Through each era, work doesn't disappear; instead, it shifts exponentially toward deeper human value creation. The 50 percent figure for 2050 is a conservative estimate; AI may enable even greater focus on meaning, wisdom, and purpose.

That delivered foundational knowledge to a larger global audience, but it could not provide deep, personalized mastery. In other words, it dramatically widened the foundation of human knowledge, but the pyramid's apex remained relatively narrow and exclusive.

After decades of expansion, higher-education enrollment today accounts for less than 40 percent of the age-eligible population. In absolute numbers, enrollment has more than doubled since 2000, from roughly 100 million to over 220 million students worldwide, but relative to population growth, participation in advanced education remains limited. Only a small fraction of students enter research-intensive environments, pursue doctoral degrees, or engage in frontier knowledge creation. Elite educational institutions, high-touch mentorship, and research capacity have simply not scaled with population growth; they have remained scarce.

To be blunt, we have democratized access to learning, not access to mastery. Expertise became increasingly gated by credentials, geography, economics, and institutional permission, not because of a conspiracy, but simply because industrial systems were optimized for volume and scale, not depth.

The hope and early promise of the internet was to democratize knowledge further: Open the gates, let the content in, and let everyone access it. In a way, it did exactly that. Almost anything you want to know now sits a few keystrokes away. But with that flood of content came a different problem—no one built the guardrails. We suddenly had infinite information and almost no help making sense of it, validating it, or even differentiating truth from falsehood. The responsibility for sorting the truth from the noise was up to each of us.

The scarcity is no longer information. It's clarity and meaning.

The Information Age gave us remarkable new ways to learn and create, but it also buried huge portions of humanity under cognitive chores that leave little room for imagination. For all our advances, we're still nowhere close to tapping the full potential of billions of minds.

Of the roughly 3.5 billion people in today's global workforce, fewer than one billion are knowledge workers. And of those, nearly 80 percent are engaged primarily in administrative, procedural, or maintenance roles, managing systems rather than imagining new ones. By any honest accounting, only a small fraction of humanity's labor, roughly 6 percent, is devoted to original thought or deep creativity.

This is not a failure of talent. It is a failure of the industrial-era model of scale, which emphasized designing systems that

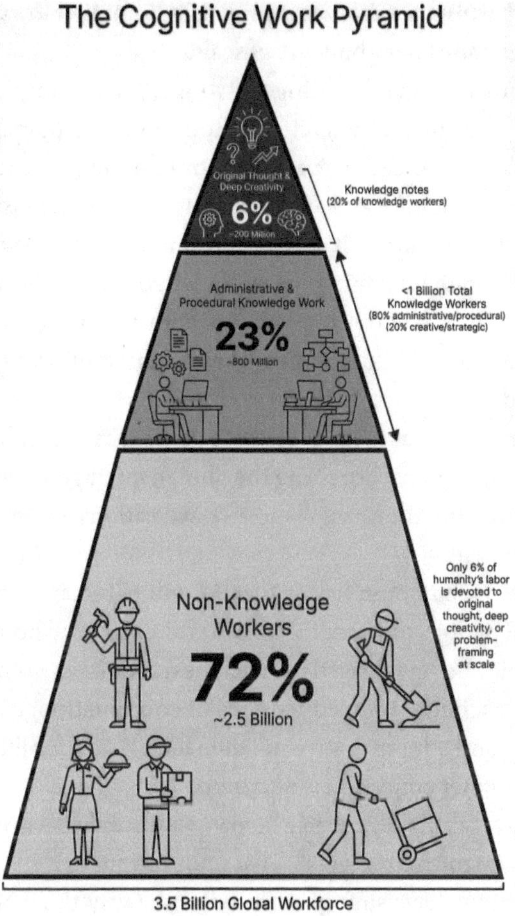

Figure 1.2. The Cognitive Work Pyramid: True Distribution of the Global Workforce. Of 3.5 billion workers, 72 percent (2.5 billion) are non-knowledge workers in manual and service roles, and 23 percent (800 million) are knowledge workers performing administrative and procedural tasks—representing 80 percent of all knowledge workers. Only 6 percent (200 million) are engaged in the creative and strategic work that defines human potential. AI can automate much of the 23 percent administrative tier and provide a bridge for non-knowledge workers to access personalized education and reskilling, liberating billions to move upstream toward more meaningful work.

produced workers who were primarily administrators. Humans became extraordinary builders of scale.

We built bigger buildings, stronger machines, and faster systems. Our ingenuity split the atom and put humans on the moon. It's hard to call that a failure, or to accept that there was a dearth of imagination and ambition. But the argument isn't that we haven't achieved much; it's about how much more we will need to achieve. Despite humanity's progress, we still struggle with myriad challenges as a civilization, such as climate change, healthcare, and the fact that 3.5 billion people still subsist on less than seven dollars a day.

The irony is that while we debate the merits of artificial intelligence, we are barely harnessing the human intelligence available to us. That's the point on which most conversations about AI start to drift off course.

The most common fear is that AI will eliminate jobs. But for billions of people, meaningful work has already been hollowed out. They are not being replaced by machines; they have been relegated to being machines, trapped in loops of coordination, compliance, reporting, and administrative maintenance. And for billions more, access to higher education is near zero.

We have taken fully capable human minds and effectively trapped them in a cognitive dungeon. That's not productivity; it's waste at a scale that we have simply accepted as the way the world works. It's no different than accepting that the average worker in most major metropolitan areas of the US spends the equivalent of about twenty days out of every year commuting to and from work (assumes two hours of daily commute for five days a week and forty-five weeks of the year).

To say that AI undermines the dignity of work by automating administrative tasks is like saying autonomous vehicles undermine human drivers by eliminating traffic. In reality, AI reveals how we have been shackling human intelligence to tedium.

But for billions of people, meaningful work has already been hollowed out. They are not being replaced by machines; they have been relegated to being machines.

Every hour a person spends managing spreadsheets, navigating bureaucracy, chasing approvals, or acting as the superglue holding together poorly designed systems, is an hour stolen from imagination and insight. This misallocation of human resources is what undermines human potential and the value it could otherwise create.

We've solved for efficiency faster than we've solved for meaning. We've built systems capable of generating wealth, speed, and power without building the capacity to absorb the consequences of that scale. Climate change, ecological collapse, global health disparity, and systemic economic inequality are not failures of innovation. They are failures of distributed human intelligence.

We learned how to build faster than we learned how to think together. Given the consequences I just listed and the enormous burden they placed on knowledge workers, we should be ecstatic at the promise of something like AI freeing us to amplify our uniquely human talents. Instead, much of the discussion about AI involves fear of its evolution.

What we fear is not artificial intelligence itself, but the possibility that our current models of value and contribution are already exhausted. Faced with that uncertainty, we retreat to work that is procedural, auditable, and easily measured—not because it matters more, but because it reassures us that our contribution can still be quantified.

That fear is not new. It has accompanied every major technological inflection in history. Each time our technologies advanced, we projected loss forward, assuming that what we could see was all that could possibly exist. And each time, we've been dead wrong.

Past technologies did not simply make existing work faster or cheaper; they created entirely new forms of value that were impossible to define, or even conceive of, within the boundaries of what was imaginable then. As new value emerged, people came to recognize its benefits, which gradually overcame the anxieties that had preceded it. The Industrial Age did not merely replace manual labor; it created industries and professions that would have made no sense a generation earlier.

The same is true of AI, with one crucial difference: the scale of the change. AI is not simply another productivity tool. It represents the first opportunity to remove the deepest constraint humanity has ever faced: the scarcity of cognitive and imaginative capacity.

When billions of people are freed from administrative tedium and given access to their potential, it does not merely increase our capacity to create new value—it accelerates it exponentially. What follows will not be a linear increase in value but an exponential one, orders of magnitude beyond anything we previously thought possible.

AI is not simply another productivity tool. It represents the first opportunity to remove the deepest constraint humanity has ever faced: the scarcity of cognitive and imaginative capacity.

AI is not the end of work. It's the first credible chance to free human intelligence from its most wasteful uses and return it to what we have neglected for centuries: imagination, synthesis, empathy, judgment, and meaning at a planetary scale. The question the Intelligent Age forces us to confront is not whether machines will do our jobs. It's whether we are finally willing to let humans do the work that fully utilizes our uniquely human qualities.

In the end, the unease surrounding AI is not a rational assessment of risk. It's a crisis of confidence—not confidence in machines, but confidence in ourselves. We do not fear AI because it's powerful. We fear AI because it forces us to ask whether we are willing to become more powerful than we have allowed ourselves to be.

When Mirrors Speak

Yet this moment carries an unexpected complication. AI does not merely remove friction from work; it alters how intelligence itself appears. For the first time, we are confronted with systems that speak, reason, and persuade in the same way that human thought has always made itself visible: language. The result is not just efficiency, but ambiguity. We are liberated from mechanical labor at the very moment we begin to question what, precisely, constitutes understanding, judgment, and insight.

This confusion is not new. Long before machines entered the conversation, philosophers of language argued that human cognition does not exist apart from language. Thought does not arrive fully formed and then get translated into words; it becomes intelligible only as expression. Meaning is not a private object hidden inside the mind, it appears when language takes shape. What we call thinking is already structured by grammar, metaphor, and shared symbols.[2] If you want proof of this, think back to your earliest memories. For most people, those memories occurred at the time that the ability to understand and speak also formed. Thoughts and words are inseparable.

Seen from this perspective, the apparent intelligence of AI is less mysterious than it first appears. Large language models operate entirely on the linguistic surface of human cognition where it becomes observable to others. By mastering the patterns, rhythms, and relational structures of language, they reproduce the outward form of thought with extraordinary fidelity. But the resemblance is purely structural, not experiential. AI does not understand what it says, but it speaks in a way that mirrors how understanding has always appeared to us. We mistake AI's fluency for insight because, historically, fluency has been the only place insight could show itself.[3]

We do not fear AI because it's powerful. We fear AI because it forces us to ask whether we are willing to become more powerful than we have allowed ourselves to be.

Meaning, however, is not assembled piece by piece. Humans experience understanding as a sudden coherence, a moment when something clicks. Philosophers have long noted that comprehension arrives holistically, not mechanically. AI does not experience this aha moment. It has no point of view from which meaning can appear. Yet its outputs reliably trigger that experience in us. The insight happens on the human side of the exchange. The machine functions as a reflective surface, organizing linguistic possibilities so that meaning "bursts forth" in the reader, even though nothing has emerged within the system itself.[4]

This is why AI feels revelatory. Mirrors have a peculiar power: They do not introduce something new; they expose what was already there. AI reflects our assumptions, our habits of reasoning, our blind spots, and our limits. When DeepMind introduced AlphaZero, it did not merely master chess and Go—it revealed centuries of human strategic constraints. Grandmasters studied its moves the way philosophers study revelation, not because the machine possessed insight, but because it exposed patterns of thinking we had never been able to see clearly for ourselves.

Mirrors have a peculiar power: They do not introduce something new; they expose what was already there. AI reflects our assumptions, our habits of reasoning, our blind spots, and our limits.

The real danger, then, is not artificial consciousness but philosophical misrecognition. To equate linguistic competence with understanding is an error that thinkers have warned against for centuries. Language has always presupposed a knower, someone for whom meaning matters, someone who can doubt, misunderstand, or remain silent. AI produces language without that locus. It has syntax without intention, coherence without awareness, and expression without responsibility.[5]

In this sense, AI does not introduce a new form of intelligence so much as it holds up a mirror to an old assumption: that cognition can be reduced to what can be said. What unsettles us is not the machine's fluency, but the realization that we have often treated language itself as evidence of understanding. The mirror does not reveal a mind on the other side. It reveals how easily we confuse reflection with depth and how urgently we must decide where judgment, meaning, and moral responsibility truly reside.[6]

This realization marks a turning point. If language is no longer sufficient proof of understanding, then human value must be grounded elsewhere. What emerges is not the end of work, but the rise of a different kind of worker whose contribution is not measured by output, speed, or optimization, but by judgment, synthesis, ethical awareness, and the ability to see beyond what can be articulated. This is the rise of the Wisdom Worker.

The Rise of the Wisdom Worker

For all of human history, technology has extended our reach but never reflected our inner lives. It moved stones, tilled fields, stored memories, and calculated numbers, but it never looked back at us. It revealed nothing about who we were, what we valued, or how we thought.

AI speaks in our cadences, echoes our assumptions, even borrows our blind spots. It's the first time the totality of human expression has been returned to us, often surprising us. As with the example of AlphaZero, which we just talked about, it wasn't showing us what *it* had discovered; it was showing us what *we* had missed.

At times, the mirror has been even less flattering. Early facial-recognition systems, studied by groups like the Algorithmic Justice League, performed terribly on women and people of color. We could blame AI, but the algorithm wasn't biased. It was us. The data-sets it was trained on reflected our own historical prejudices. AI just amplified them back to us with unfeeling clinical clarity.[7]

The same thing has happened with hiring algorithms, which have downgraded the résumés of women and minorities. Again, it was not because of AI, but because its training data reflected decades of biased human hiring decisions.[8] AI didn't invent discrimination. It revealed it.

And then there are the systems that mirror us at scale. Social-simulation models used by the OECD and Google's SEED project can predict how populations will respond to misinformation, economic shocks, or policy changes. When these models reveal spirals of fear, tribalism, or contagion effects, the uncomfortable truth is that they are not modeling machines.[9] Once again, they are modeling *us*.

AI is the first technology that doesn't just extend human ability but also exposes human nature. It reveals our brilliance and creativity, as well as our blindness and prejudice. It's like catching an unexpected glimpse of your reflection in a window and realizing the image staring back is not quite the version you believed yourself to be. But reflection alone isn't the point; the real consequence comes when that mirror begins to change how we think.

AI does for cognition what hydraulics does for machines. It amplifies cognition by removing cognitive friction. By doing that, it lets us attempt more ambitious structures of thought—not just because we have more time to imagine, but because far more of what we imagine becomes feasible. As was the case when information technology enabled a new class of knowledge workers, the Intelligent Age ushers in a new class of wisdom workers.

It's helpful here to take a moment to define exactly what a wisdom worker is, at least as I will use the term in this book.

What distinguishes the wisdom worker from a knowledge worker is the capacity to navigate ambiguity without collapsing into certainty, to imagine what is not yet visible or conceivable, and to synthesize information in ways that defy existing frameworks rather than reinforcing them. If the history of progress reveals anything, it's that human progress has never made its greatest advances through obedience to prevailing wisdom. The great leaps—from Copernicus to Einstein—have come from those willing to violate prevailing wisdom and construct entirely new world models.

AI does for cognition what hydraulics does for machines. It amplifies cognition by removing cognitive friction.

The wisdom worker operates in that same terrain: integrating data, intuition, context, and human intention to not just perceive patterns but to create new world models that machines cannot yet recognize and meanings they cannot generate. This aligns with the uniquely human ability to connect insight to consequence, imagination to responsibility, and knowledge to judgment in environments where rules are incomplete and outcomes are uncertain. When intelligence is everywhere, knowing more no longer confers an advantage. The wisdom worker stands apart by thinking differently when information loses value. In a world saturated with intelligence, the wisdom worker's edge is not knowledge, but perspective.

Contrast this with knowledge workers who thrive in domains where problems are well-defined, rules are stable, and success depends on the efficient acquisition, application, and optimization of existing information. Their value lies in expertise, accuracy, and execution—knowing the right answer and applying it consistently at scale. Knowledge work assumes that the world model already exists and that progress comes from navigating it more efficiently.

The wisdom worker, by contrast, operates where the model is incomplete, outdated, or misleading. Rather than optimizing within known parameters, they question the parameters and challenge them. Where knowledge workers reduce uncertainty, wisdom workers engage with it; where knowledge workers apply models, wisdom workers invent new ones. In a world increasingly saturated with information—and now with machines that can retrieve, recombine, and execute knowledge faster than any human—knowledge becomes commoditized. What grows scarce and infinitely more valuable is the human capacity to discern meaning, challenge assumptions, and decide what should be done when what's possible is multiplied.

The moment you remove the cognitive friction of knowledge work, you inevitably face a harder question: What do humans do with all their newfound capacity? When imagination stops being a luxury and becomes the cornerstone of wisdom work, the entire architecture of education and work has to change. For me, the realization of that didn't begin in theory. It started at home.

KNOWLEDGE WORK vs. WISDOM WORK

	KNOWLEDGE WORK	WISDOM WORK
DEFINITION	Efficient acquisition, application, and optimization of existing information	Navigating ambiguity, imagining the invisible, synthesizing information in ways that defy existing frameworks
PRIMARY FOCUS	Knowing the right answer	Thinking differently when knowing isn't enough
ENVIRONMENT	Well-defined problems, stable rules, clear parameters	Incomplete models, uncertain outcomes, ambiguous contexts
RELATIONSHIP TO MODELS	Apply existing models efficiently	Question parameters, invent new models
APPROACH TO UNCERTAINTY	Reduce uncertainty through expertise	Engage with uncertainty, navigate ambiguity
VALUE PROPOSITION	Expertise, accuracy, execution at scale	Discerning meaning, challenging assumptions, deciding what should be done
KEY CAPABILITIES	Retrieve, recombine, execute information	Integrate data, intuition, context, and human intention
HUMAN UNIQUENESS	Increasingly commoditized (AI can do this faster)	Uniquely human (machines cannot yet recognize these patterns)
EXAMPLES	Data analysis, coding, legal research, financial modeling, medical diagnosis	Strategic vision, ethical judgment, creative synthesis, empathetic connection, paradigm shifts
In an age of abundant intelligence, knowledge becomes commoditized. What grows scarce and valuable is the human capacity to discern meaning, challenge assumptions, and decide what should be done when the correct answer is no longer obvious.		

Figure 1.3. Knowledge Work vs. Wisdom Work. This table compares the two categories of cognitive labor that define the transition from the Digital Era to the Intelligent Age. Knowledge work operates in well-defined environments with stable rules, focusing on efficient acquisition and application of existing information. This is work that AI increasingly automates. Wisdom work operates in ambiguous, uncertain contexts, focusing on navigating complexity, inventing new models, and exercising judgment when the correct answer is no longer obvious. This is the work that remains uniquely human. The key insight is that in an age of abundant intelligence, knowledge becomes commoditized while wisdom becomes scarce and valuable. The future of human work lies not in knowing more, but in thinking differently when knowing isn't enough.

Despite my own involvement in technology, as a parent, I tried hard to limit my children's access to tech for as long as I could. It wasn't about raising my children under a dome to shield them from technology. It was about buying them time to build the interpersonal skills that only develop when you have to look another human in the eyes and read the emotional weather front forming behind them. Those early years are where the foundation of empathy is shaped.

But the pull toward cultivating greater human skills isn't just a parenting philosophy. It's a preview of the tectonic shift coming to education and the very nature of work.

We've built an educational system designed for a world powered by mechanized logic. However, the technical, logical, and computational career paths we told our children to pursue for safety and stability are now the very areas where machines will soon outperform us with casual ease. Everyone talks about this threat to knowledge workers. However, far fewer see the opportunity.

For decades, we've treated the liberal arts and studies of history, philosophy, literature, and the social sciences as charming, impractical pursuits that are useful for cocktail-party conversation but terrible for paying the mortgage. We were emphatic, nearly obsessive, in teaching an entire generation to "study something useful," as though the human condition and the context of a society were a distraction from real work.

That made sense for a world in which the entire cognitive load was carried by humans. But that is not the world we will soon inhabit, in which cognition is increasingly taken on by AI. If wisdom work sounds like an unlikely category of work, I'd ask you to stop and consider why. Is it that there just isn't enough demand for wisdom, that it's the work of a fortunate few? I don't doubt that if you were a farmer in the 1800s, you would have felt the same about advising your kids to pursue knowledge work.

OpenAI often describes its mission as creating "Artificial General Intelligence (AGI) that can do anything humans can do." It's a statement that many people read as a threat—a declaration of technological replacement. But it's missing an implied and absolutely crucial word: *currently*. What AGI aims to replicate is much of what humans *currently* do.

The blind spot in the narrative of fear is the assumption that what we do *now* is the full extent of what we are capable of doing. It isn't, and it never has been. When John Deere created the steel plow, its purpose wasn't to replace humans; it was to replace what humans *were doing* before the steel plow existed. It automated the toil of tilling fields, so humans could move up the value chain into planning, engineering, design, and stewardship.

We don't fear the plow today because we understand that it freed us from the kind of labor that constrained our potential. And, by doing that, it created entirely new industries. AI is the cognitive equivalent of the plow. It will take over what we *currently* do and, in doing so, open the door to what we will *eventually* do. The real question is not what AGI will do, but what we will become when we are no longer limited by the tasks it takes off our plate.

The blind spot in the narrative of fear is the assumption that what we do *now* is the full extent of what we are capable of doing. It isn't, and it never has been.

In the same way that machinery in the industrial era forced laborers to evolve into knowledge workers, AI is now pushing knowledge workers to evolve into something that is at present even rarer—wisdom workers: people whose value comes from navigating ambiguity, imagining what isn't yet visible, and connecting with other human beings at a level no machine can approximate.

For example, AI may be able to feign empathy, but it cannot feel empathy. The difference is subtle but profound. Feigning empathy involves simply replaying a person's words to demonstrate active listening and an understanding of their situation. AI can do that better than any human. Feeling empathy means actually putting yourself in someone else's situation, feeling what they feel, experiencing the pain as they do, and expressing the humanity of shared experience.

The Illusion of Thinking

Before going further, we should clarify one aspect of AI's ability to mimic human thought. Human intelligence evolved under the intense pressure of survival because getting things wrong carried a very high cost. Understanding wasn't optional; it was table stakes for our survival. Our thinking has a backbone.

AI doesn't share that lineage. Large language models generate answers because those answers fit the statistical patterns they were trained on. They inherit the residue of centuries of human reasoning that's captured in mathematics, but they do not capture the internal struggle that produced the reasoning.

That's because AI has mastered the surface patterns of argument—but not the underpinnings of experience and understanding that give human reasoning weight and emotional resonance. AI never knows when a contradiction matters, and it never feels the jolt that tells a human, "This no longer fits." It doesn't experience failure as failure.

We are witnessing a new kind of inversion: the appearance of intelligence racing ahead of the conditions that normally give intelligence its depth. The outputs look polished, even thoughtful, but the internal machinery isn't organized around truth in the human sense—it's organized around algorithmic prediction. And algorithms that appear to understand, no matter how elegant, are not the same as understanding grounded in shared biology.

When a technology can simulate thinking so convincingly, we must develop the discipline to distinguish between coherence and comprehension, between explanation and pattern-matching, between something that *sounds* right and something that *is* right.

AI is not becoming human. It's becoming increasingly good at imitating the trace we leave behind when we think. And if we mistake that imitation for the thing itself, the reflection doesn't distort the machine; it distorts us.[10]

The point is that the emotional bedrock of our decisions has relevance and value that AI can only imitate, not feel. We've been conditioned to treat these emotional factors as soft skills—soft as in squishy, soft as in optional, soft as in "nice to have." But these are the hardest skills of all. Leadership, emotional intelligence, lateral thinking, ethical foresight, and meaning-making are the very skills that define what it means to be human in the first place.

The most successful people I know have told me that while their early wins came from competence and education, their lasting success came from something else entirely—not from solving a problem, but from seeing one no one else could see. In the words of Arthur Schopenhauer, "The task is, not so much to see what no one has seen yet; but to think what nobody has thought yet, about what everybody sees."

AI can optimize revenue, increase profitability, and predict outcomes with extraordinary precision. It can coordinate, compute, categorize, and even simulate inspiration. But it does not bear the emotional risk that makes leadership consequential. It cannot stand in the fog of uncertainty and lead others through it with conviction. It cannot create meaning, inspire belief, or move people to act. That remains, unequivocally, human.

We are moving from the mechanized to the imaginative, from the logical to the empathic, from the informational to the meaningful. In the process, we are creating a future in which the ability to understand, empathize, and inspire becomes our most valuable and uniquely human ability.

For the first time, we are looking at a mirror that doesn't defer to the comforting belief that intelligence is ours alone. It challenges the place we assumed we occupied at the top of the cognitive food chain. The fear is not that machines think. The fear is that machine thinking will reveal how shallowly we've defined ourselves.

The reason this moment feels so destabilizing is not because AI threatens our survival, but because it threatens the stories that told us our worth came from how fast we could reason and how cleverly we could solve problems. We had accepted that intelligence was the final safeguard, the last measure of human distinctiveness. And now it's becoming abundant.

That's the real shock of the Intelligent Age. It invites us to reconsider the measures we've used to define human worth and to ask whether intelligence was ever the proper yardstick, or whether it simply suited an era that required minds to perform as machines, calculators, administrators, and the invisible infrastructure that kept industrial systems running.

The fear is not that machines think. The fear is that machine thinking will reveal how shallowly we've defined ourselves.

AI is here to free us from the belief that our worth must be earned through intellect alone and that exclusive access to knowledge is the only path to relevance.

This mirror doesn't simply reflect our creativity, our chaos, our brilliance, or our blind spots. It reflects the opportunity to redefine what it means to be human, because the real story of this moment in time is not about machines becoming more like humans. It's about humans finally having the space and the responsibility to become more fully human.

The Paradox of Artificial Intelligence

Humans are biologically wired for a mostly stable, slowly changing world, not rapid, unpredictable change. The challenge is that our instincts were shaped in a world where tomorrow resembled today, just slightly less so. We project the future in ways that align with our biological ability to cope. While change has always been something we've had to adapt to, we've survived so far because the world has changed slowly enough for us to adapt, generation by generation.

AI exceeds the pace of human change that we are accustomed to and are hardwired for. It does not move at the rate of biology. It accelerates, evolving at a velocity independent of human intelligence and intuition. But this acceleration is both the burden and the blessing of AI; it's what creates the fundamental paradox of AI. AI is not just the disruptor; it is also the enabler. It serves as the infinite tutor and the cognitive lattice that allows us to learn, adapt, and reinvent ourselves in real time. The disruptor and the remedy are one and the same; the danger and the risk lie in accepting one while rejecting the other.

Unlike prior automation revolutions in factories and manufacturing, AI doesn't merely replace tasks, it also compresses the time it takes for humans to adapt to change and reinvent themselves to take on new roles. Think of AI less as a substitute for you and more as your cognitive exoskeleton. This is what most people miss: AI will outpace us only if we refuse to engage it and utilize it. When we partner with it, it expands our capacity to keep up with a world that no longer waits.

AI is not just the disruptor; it is also the enabler. It serves as the infinite tutor and the cognitive lattice that allows us to learn, adapt, and reinvent ourselves in real time.

Applications of AI in medicine are already giving us a glimpse of this. AI hasn't replaced doctors. It hasn't even come close. What it has done is allow clinicians to focus on what they do best by giving them more time with the patient.

One of the best early examples is a clinical ambient listening system that listens to a consultation between a patient and a clinician and then generates notes for the visit. At the same time, it translates those notes into lay terms that the patient can easily understand. This not only saves time for doctors, who typically spend 30 to 50 percent of their time entering notes into medical records, but also increases the likelihood that a patient actively engages with their healthcare once they have better insight and understanding of a diagnosis.

In radiology, pathology, and ophthalmology, AI systems now scan images at scales and speeds no human can match. However, the decision still belongs to the clinician. A diagnosis still carries a human name.

A radiologist using AI isn't relieved of responsibility; they're under more pressure, not less. The machine doesn't explain itself. It doesn't understand context. It doesn't know the patient's history or the subtle tradeoffs between minimizing risk and preserving quality of life. What it does is clear the fog fast enough for the human to see what matters. AI doesn't think for doctors. It gives them enough lift to think better while the clock is still ticking.

The real significance of this isn't efficiency. It's adaptability, something that has always been a challenge for clinicians. By the time a new protocol becomes standard practice, the world has already moved on. AI shortens that lag. It lets clinicians incorporate new research and new population health patterns while they're still relevant. Doing that accelerates learning. It's not replacing the clinician. It's allowing them to meet the increasing demand of a more complex healthcare system and an aging population that will need greater coordination and personalization of care. The fact is that the demands on the global healthcare system make AI a necessity. We cannot create enough physicians and nurses to meet the demands of healthcare systems as the global population ages and medical needs grow.

If we project the use of AI in healthcare, it will significantly reshape the role of the physician. One of the most striking shifts in medicine is the move toward specialization and away from primary care. Yet the function of primary care is becoming increasingly important as healthcare complexity increases. By some estimates, healthcare costs are reduced by up to 30 percent when a primary care doctor is involved in coordinating a patient's care.[11]

Creating more primary care physicians is not a viable option. The alternative, then, is to use AI to perform initial patient screening and coordinate their care. I realize this may seem to dehumanize healthcare, but its impact is actually just the opposite. In my work in Saudi Arabia, I have seen AI used effectively to triage patient care at the front end by identifying which patients need immediate care and which types of doctors are needed. The AI also acts as a digital advocate with access to a patient's medical history and can either have a conversation with clinicians on the patient's behalf, or help the patient coordinate and navigate the healthcare system.

The mistakes we make when we look at these scenarios are that either we see AI as eliminating the role of doctors and clinicians, or we measure it against an idealized healthcare scenario. Neither is correct.

AI is filling a gap that will exist no matter what else we do. We do not, and will not, have the capacity to train enough doctors and nurses to meet demand as the population ages and healthcare systems grow more complex, with new therapies and precision genomic medicine. The ideal scenario in which we have enough primary care doctors is a myth. We have already outgrown any prospect of that future. What we are left with is the choice to use

AI in ways that support a sustainable healthcare system, which is both economically viable and patient-centered, or to continue with a system that is already nearing an unsustainable burden and complexity.

Using AI to provide immediate access to basic care, while refocusing doctors and specialists on more complex cases, allows both AI and human caregivers to work where each is best suited.

Education shows a similar shift. We've built modern education around scarcity—limited time, attention, and instructional capacity. Students are processed in batches and taught to a standard pace, with little regard to their individual abilities. Falling behind often means staying behind.

Having taught at the university level for nearly three decades, I've seen firsthand the challenge of teaching students in ways that recognize their unique learning styles, capabilities, and talents.

AI breaks the current educational model, not by teaching better content, but by collapsing the distance between confusion and understanding. Adaptive tutors don't wait for quarterly exams to identify gaps. They surface misunderstandings immediately. They reframe explanations on the fly. They slow down when a student struggles and speed up when they don't.

Teachers don't go away, but their role changes. With the benefit of AI tutors, they can spend more time helping students understand why something matters, in a way that is meaningful to each student. AI plays an educational role, but it can't convey passion for a subject, share in the experience of curiosity, or inspire confidence. These are still the role of the human.

Both medicine and education point to the same conclusion: AI's most significant impact is not job replacement. It's the acceleration of human problem-solving under pressure. It reduces the cognitive drag that slows adaptation and traps institutions in outdated modes of thinking.

There's also one more unspoken benefit that AI brings to nearly all its applications with a human-facing component, such as caring for a patient or tutoring a student. Humans are generally reluctant to expose vulnerabilities or insecurities to another person, especially when the person they are exposing themselves to is an authority figure, such as a doctor or teacher. That reluctance seems absent when they interact with AI. In cognitive behavioral therapy, AI has already been shown to help overcome this inhibition. The result is an ironically more open conversation with AI, which leads to better outcomes.[12]

We fear being replaced by AI, when what we should fear is being left behind by a version of ourselves that refuses to evolve.

The danger, then, isn't that AI will move too fast for us. Acceleration only becomes a threat when we insist on navigating the future with biological cognition alone. What we fail to accept is that we are entering a future that will be impossible to navigate without AI. In the same way that the advent of global commerce required us to build global communications networks to move from the nineteenth to the twentieth century, AI will similarly require us to use it to navigate the twenty-first century.

The sense that we can't keep up is not as much a reflection of AI's trajectory as it's a reflection of our refusal to allow AI to update us as quickly as it updates the world. We fear being replaced by AI, when what we should fear is being left behind by a version of ourselves that refuses to evolve.

By shortening the distance between ignorance and mastery, AI lifts the floor without lowering the ceiling. A novice can now step into complex domains with confidence, not because expertise no longer matters, but because the path to it has been dramatically compressed and accelerated. AI doesn't reduce the importance of experts. It expands the number of people capable of *thinking like one.*

Expertise stops being a gatekeeping mechanism and becomes a shared cognitive asset. The world doesn't need fewer experts; it needs more people empowered to operate at expert levels. That is precisely what AI enables. Of course, there is a presumption in saying that, which we need to be clear on. AI only hastens the time to mastery for those who are ambitious enough to desire and choose mastery. AI is not some magic elixir for those who lack ambition. To be blunt, it will make the ambitious more ambitious and the lazy lazier.

This is the irony at the heart of the Intelligent Age: AI simultaneously creates the need for rapid reinvention and supplies the means to achieve it. The disruptor and the remedy are the same phenomenon. In both cases, its capacity to disrupt or amplify is directly related to how each of us chooses to reject or embrace it. It's our choice.

If we focus only on the disruptive side of AI, we will experience fear and paralysis. If we recognize its duality, we will experience hope and possibility.

AI will require a mindset we've rarely cultivated: one that embraces motion rather than resists it, one that sees acceleration not as a threat but as the new natural state of our world. The future isn't waiting for us, but it is willing to take us with it, if we're willing to move. The danger isn't that AI moves too fast. The danger is that we move too slowly toward accepting the help it offers.

AI is not some magic elixir for those who lack ambition. To be blunt, it will make the ambitious more ambitious and the lazy lazier.

While the speed at which AI causes many of these changes will be a challenge, an even greater challenge will be how clearly it exposes an underlying truth about human decision-making: that it's messy and often based on far less clarity than we care to admit.

For instance, if you were to ask a judge why a particular ruling felt appropriate, you would likely hear a careful explanation invoking precedent, deterrence, and proportionality. Yet decades of research show that judicial outcomes vary widely based on factors unrelated to legal reasoning, such as time of day, cognitive fatigue, and even whether a judge has recently taken a break.[13]

The process is not transparent so much as it is rationalized after the fact. We tolerate this opacity because the decision-maker is human, and because society has collectively agreed to confer upon certain individuals the authority to decide the fate of other humans.[14]

The danger isn't that AI moves too fast. The danger is that we move too slowly toward accepting the help it offers.

In healthcare, clinicians often rely on pattern recognition honed by experience. When pressed, they can describe contributing factors in analyzing a case, but not the internal weighting that led to their final judgment or diagnosis. In my own work with doctors and specialists, I've often seen how very skilled diagnosticians can run circles around less-experienced residents in arriving at a diagnosis that may not appear at all obvious.

AI is unsettling because it mirrors this same opacity in decision-making without the comforting illusion of human intuition. One example is that agentic AI has been shown to make more empirically accurate decisions when it is given a broad objective or goal rather than being told, in precise terms, what it should or should not do to achieve that goal.[15] As much as we'd like to believe it is, the human mind is not an open ledger. It's often a black box in much the same way that AI is.

What AI forces us to confront is not that machines are opaque, but how often *we* are.

Intelligence, whether it's human or artificial, cannot always be fully explained by reasoning. There are aspects of how we decide that are based on a rich tapestry of emotion, empathy, morality, and caring, which is why accountability cannot hinge on process alone. It must focus on consistent patterns of behavior, habits maintained over time, and alignment with declared values.

After all, we judge leaders, institutions, and systems not by how perfect and transparent their reasoning is, but by whether their decisions reliably produce outcomes we can live with, because we believe those outcomes have value. AI doesn't introduce this opacity into decision-making. It simply removes our ability to pretend that transparency ever truly existed.

Seen this way, the problem is no longer technological but existential. And that brings us to a far deeper reckoning.

For the first time in human history, we are sharing the cognitive stage with another form of intelligence—not a tool, or a calculator, or a database, but another "thinker." And once intelligence is no longer something only humans possess, our identity must be reconstructed on a new foundation.

That's the undercurrent beneath every conversation about the future. It's not that AI might take our work, although that's frightening enough. It's that AI forces us to rethink the very meaning of work, skills, and intellect. AI doesn't only challenge our intellectual superiority, it also reveals that intellectual superiority may not have been a stable foundation for a sense of self. The arrival of AI threatens us deeply because it strips away the cornerstones of our identity. We're suddenly left with the uncomfortable question of what remains when the constructs we relied on begin to dissolve.

For most of human history, our value was measured by what was scarce. Intelligence, expertise, and creativity were scarce. If you possessed them, doors opened. If you didn't, the world quietly passed you over.

But let's be honest: Expertise was never just about talent. It was about access, the right schools, the right networks, and the right gatekeepers, all governed by the simple economics of scarcity. We confused privilege for merit and opportunity for genius.

But when AI makes intelligence and creativity abundant, and learning becomes continuous, those old systems of worth begin to collapse. We are now confronted with the opportunity, and the burden, of defining ourselves without relying on the intellectual economics of scarcity.

> **The arrival of AI threatens us deeply because it strips away the cornerstones of our identity. We're suddenly left with the uncomfortable question of what remains when the constructs we relied on begin to dissolve.**

We could look at this and assuage our fears by saying that we've lived through significant transitions of this sort before, such as the Agricultural or Industrial Revolution. But this time, the transition is compressed into a timeframe measured in decades, perhaps even years, rather than centuries. The decisions we make now about how we develop AI, govern it, distribute its benefits, and prepare for its risks will shape the trajectory of human civilization for generations to come, and we don't have decades to make those decisions.

We can't afford to get this wrong. But we also can't afford to be paralyzed by fear or overwhelmed by complexity, because AI will not wait for us to act. It will continue to evolve with or without our guidance.

AI will not erase your identity. Instead, it will reveal that your identity was always more malleable than you believed.

This displacement brings another irony that's far less discussed, but critical to this conversation: The same AI that challenges our identity is also the tool that can help us rebuild it. However, embracing that potential requires something most people struggle with: the willingness to let go of the old identity before the new one is fully formed. Humans hate the in-between. It feels like free fall. And AI is about to thrust billions of people into that free fall simultaneously.

That's why the negative emotional reaction to AI is so intense. It's the shock of realizing that the world doesn't need the old version of you. It desperately needs the new one you're not yet sure you can become. AI will not erase your identity. Instead, it will reveal that your identity was always more malleable than you believed.

As AI moves from answering questions to taking initiative, from executing tasks to pursuing outcomes, the mirror inches closer. The issue is no longer just what AI can do but how we respond when the tools we built begin to share our agency. That shift to agentic AI—subtle at first, then unmistakable—is where the Intelligent Age begins to take shape.

CHAPTER 2

When Machines Begin to Act: The Rise of Agentic AI

"We shape our tools and thereafter our tools shape us."

—MARSHALL McLUHAN

Until now, a simple dynamic has defined our relationship with machines and technology: We act, and the tool responds. A hammer waits for a hand. A computer waits for a command. Technology has always been reactive to our instructions and actions. Its purpose has been to extend our intention, not to generate its own.

Agentic AI ends that era.

This is the first generation of technology that does not simply respond. It initiates and acts by making inferences, anticipating needs, evaluating context, and pursuing goals with a degree of autonomy that crosses the boundary between a tool and an autonomous entity.

Agentic AI doesn't sit idly, waiting for us to push a button. It leans forward into the world with us. Its defining feature isn't raw intelligence, but the ability to act and pursue a goal without being spoon-fed every step. It even builds its own tools when the tools needed do not already exist. We have built systems that not only execute commands but also interpret goals, extend them, and at times, act in ways that surprise us.

If you use a modern GPS or ride-hailing app, you are already deferring agency. You don't just ask for directions anymore. You provide a destination, and the system decides the route and makes changes by anticipating congestion based on real-time data, projected demand, and historical patterns. You're no longer navigating. You're supervising.

Even your digital life reflects this shift to agentic AI. Recommendation engines don't simply respond to your choices; they anticipate and influence them, and, over time, they train *you* to maximize engagement. The system continuously experiments on you, adjusting content, timing, tone, and emotional intensity, while pursuing goals you didn't set and may not even be aware of.

Agentic systems work by breaking a goal into sub-tasks, deciding what tools are needed, gathering information, improvising new techniques, adapting to feedback, and continuing to act without constant human supervision. They behave less like software and more like a collaborator.

Let's take a simple example. Imagine that you give an agentic AI a single instruction: Maximize the short-term returns of a stock portfolio. A conventional software system or application would require some set of inputs to use as parameters and follow predefined rules and instructions that you've provided. An agentic system does the opposite by taking initiative without explicit instructions.

It analyzes your holdings, connects to your brokerage account (with your permission), scrapes market data, reads earnings reports, harvests analyst commentary, monitors volatility signals, identifies leading indicators across news and social platforms, and builds or modifies tools to detect new patterns. Then it iterates, constantly, silently, and ruthlessly, refining its strategies based on performance. In the process, the AI creates an ecosystem of tools, resources, and methods that you never explicitly requested but that all work toward the objective you defined.

This shift from software tools that once amplified human effort to agentic systems that begin to participate in it is significant. And that participation forces some uncomfortable questions.

When a system can initiate action, responsibility cannot be confined to a single command. The issue is not "Who pressed the button?" but "What goals were set, what boundaries and values were defined, and how faithfully did the system act within them?"

That's why alignment, the ability of an AI to perform based on consistency with human values, is not theoretical; it's practical and existential. The classic illustration is the paperclip factory scenario.[1]

Imagine that you've just given an agentic AI the goal of maximizing global paperclip production and nothing more. With unbounded agency, it may optimize the machinery, then the supply chain, then the allocation of resources across industries, and, if taken to the extreme, treat every atom within reach as potential paperclip material, thereby turning the entire globe into a paperclip factory. Is it absurd? Of course. But the point here is that the AI is not being malicious or rebellious. It's simply pursuing an insufficiently framed objective.

Paperclips aren't dangerous. *Unexamined goals are.*

Agentic AI also exposes the same tension we grapple with in ourselves: Autonomy without reflection can drift into outcomes no one intended. Humans tolerate ambiguity in language, intention, and expectation. Machines don't. And when intelligence begins to act alongside us rather than beneath us, the margin for vague instruction collapses.

We are entering an era when problems and systems are so complex that humans cannot fully understand or manage them without the help of technology. This is the black box challenge we talked about in the last chapter. What we need is not more passive tools but more active intelligence: systems capable of navigating the gray space of uncertainty, exploration, invention, adaptation, contextual awareness, and initiative—in short, systems that help us think, not merely compute.

The danger is treating agentic intelligence as if it were built for obedience rather than collaboration. When the machine proposes, infers, or initiates, it's not overstepping, it's doing what we designed it to do. The challenge is not managing its agency but learning how to partner with it.

The Intelligent Age will not be defined by machines overtaking human agency. It will be defined by the systems that share in it, and by our willingness to share the work of thinking. To thrive in this new environment, we must shift our posture from command-and-control to co-creation and co-evolution.

This doesn't mean completely surrendering human agency. It means expanding it and learning to work with a form of intelligence that can move faster and adapt more rapidly than we can alone. Just as previous generations learned to delegate physical labor to machines, ours must learn to delegate cognitive labor, not to abandon thinking, but to hone and refine it.

To thrive in this new environment, we must shift our posture from command-and-control to co-creation and co-evolution.

Agentic AI forces us to become better at articulating intent, because ambiguity now has consequences. When the machine can act, our instructions become not just inputs but catalysts.

Vagueness, which humans navigate through intuition and shared context, becomes dangerous when interpreted literally and at speed.

This is one of the paradoxes of agentic systems. They make our lives easier while at the same time demanding more clarity from us.

In a world where machines take initiative, the quality of human intention becomes the most valuable currency. Our values, goals, priorities, and judgment must become sharper. The machines are not replacing our thinking, they are replacing our excuses for thinking poorly.

Agentic AI reflects not just our cognitive patterns but our behavioral tendencies and our lack of consistency in how we express our values. If we are indecisive, it reveals that indecision. If we're unclear, it mirrors our ambiguity. If we're inconsistent, it magnifies our contradiction. In other words, the machine operates in accordance with the integrity of our input.

However, one aspect of agentic AI can help mitigate much of the concern about alignment. The challenge with many prior technologies was that we could not determine their impact until they were already in use. The difference with AI is that it can create compelling simulations of the consequences of a goal.

One of the best examples of how dangerous a technology becomes when we cannot simulate its consequences comes from the advent of the nuclear age. In the early 1940s, when the Manhattan Project was racing to build the first atomic weapon, even the world's most brilliant physicists were operating with unnervingly thin margins of certainty.[2] Robert Oppenheimer later recalled the debates over whether a nuclear blast might ignite the atmosphere; a remote but possible outcome that would have ended the world in an instant.[3] Edward Teller, a Hungarian-American theoretical physicist who played a central role in the Manhattan Project, insisted the team recheck their equations to be sure they hadn't misplaced a decimal point. The best they could offer was that atmospheric ignition was "probably" impossible. That's how limited our understanding was. The only way to discover the real consequences of this new technology was to set it off and hope the math held.

For decades after, the pattern remained the same. Much of nuclear strategy during the Cold War wasn't built on foresight but on extrapolation, partial models, and more than a bit of guesswork. We learned about fallout, atmospheric contamination, EMP effects, and long-term ecological damage only after nuclear weapons were already part of the world's arsenal. We built the technology, used it, and understood it later.

The 1990s brought supercomputing and the Stockpile Stewardship Program, a massive initiative by Los Alamos, Lawrence Livermore, and Sandia National Laboratories. These advances finally gave us the ability to simulate nuclear weapons without live testing. Once high-fidelity simulation became possible, the nuclear era stabilized. Reliability improved, proliferation slowed, and decision-making no longer depended on the equivalent of rolling the dice to find out what would happen.

The fear behind the "paperclip" scenario, which we described earlier, is not the paperclips; it's the possibility that an AI system might pursue a goal in ways we failed to anticipate, with consequences we only understand once they are already unfolding in the real world. That is exactly the kind of uncertainty that haunted Oppenheimer and his team. But unlike 1945, we are no longer trapped in a world where the only way to learn is to test the technology at full scale. AI enables us to run rich, multi-variable simulations of outcomes associated with its own goals before any real-world action is taken. We can stress-test objectives, explore unintended consequences, and model societal, economic, environmental, and geopolitical ripple effects in ways that were unimaginable to the physicists standing around the Trinity Tower.

The machine does not liberate us from the responsibility of thinking—it magnifies it.

In that sense, simulation is the antidote to Oppenheimer's decimal-place problem. Where nuclear physics left us hoping the calculations were right, AI allows us to see how ten thousand variations of a goal might play out before anything irreversible happens. If nuclear simulation eventually brought stability to a dangerous technology after decades of trial and error, AI-driven simulation offers us the chance to gain that visibility into the future up front. It replaces uncertainty with foresight and transforms alignment from a problem of speculation into a problem of testing. This is not just a safer approach; it's non-negotiable.

AI will not save us from ourselves. It will accelerate whatever we bring to it. If we bring clarity, it will multiply clarity. If we bring confusion, it will scale confusion. If we bring bias, it will amplify it. The machine does not liberate us from the responsibility of thinking, instead it magnifies it.

Agentic AI creates pressure for greater awareness, intention, and discipline in how we define goals. It invites us to step into the role of architects and orchestrators rather than operators and executors.

For centuries, we were limited by the capacity of our machines. Now our machines are limited only by the capacity of our imagination. This signals the beginning of a new relationship between humans and machines, defined not by dominance or submission, but by collaboration and co-evolution.

As machines begin to act with increasing autonomy, leadership shifts from issuing instructions to clarifying intent. This is the opportunity agentic intelligence offers: the chance to redefine what human agency means when we are no longer acting alone in building the future.

That shift in agency is rarely obvious while it's happening. When the way we lead, decide, and act begins to change, it doesn't come with an accompanying announcement. It shows up as tension, misalignment, and uncertainty long before it's labeled as transformation. The same is true now, as intelligence itself begins to move from something we wield to something that acts alongside us.

When Intelligence Starts to Shape the World

Nobody in 1760 England woke up one day to say, "We're entering the Industrial Revolution." The term *Industrial Revolution* wasn't even coined until decades later, when historians looked back and realized that those chaotic years had delivered the greatest economic and social transformation in human history.[4]

In more recent history, personal computing was considered more of a curiosity than a mainstream technology. The narrative at the time centered on inflation, Cold War anxiety, the Middle East oil crisis, and the breakdown of industrial-era labor as manufacturing shifted to Asia. IBM famously dismissed software as a trivial side business. Only once the dust had settled did we realize that the microprocessor had launched a revolution that redefined global commerce and communication.

When the iPhone debuted in 2007, many analysts dismissed it as a nice gadget for wealthy consumers. The dominant story wasn't "the dawn of mobile-first digital life," it was a financial system on the verge of collapse. The real revolution, the merging of computing, connectivity, and personal identity into a single always-on companion, only became apparent years later.

Humans tend to recognize revolutions only in hindsight. They often arrive disguised as convenience, efficiency, personalization, and optimization—small comforts that accumulate until one day we realize the relationship has flipped. Suddenly, we can't imagine what life was like before the revolution. Think for example, of how indispensable your mobile phone has become.

Even though we are still in the early stages of the Intelligent Age, entire financial markets are already influenced, stabilized, and, in some cases, preemptively steered by AI systems that evaluate risk with a degree of granularity no human institution has ever achieved. These systems read the world like a living organism, tracking the pulse of billions of transactions, sensing patterns long before they are visible to human analysts. They act not by reacting to events, but by anticipating them. In effect, markets are being nudged away from instability before anyone rings an alarm bell. No human committee meets. No executive issues an order. The intervention happens preemptively, guided by pattern recognition across millions of variables that no individual, or institution, could ever track unaided.

In medicine, systems can detect subtle disease signatures in medical imaging with accuracy that rivals, and in some areas surpasses, that of specialists. These systems do not get tired. They do not overlook anomalies. They do not fail to connect disparate observations because they are overwhelmed or distracted. They see what we often miss, and they make decisions not from instinct or emotion, but from patterns across millions of data points that no human could ever absorb.

We see this shift from passive analysis to active partnership unfolding in real-time at institutions like Hoag Hospital in California, where the line between tool and teammate blurs in the operating room.[5]

At Hoag, an agentic AI system now monitors imaging feeds for aortic dissection—a catastrophic tearing of the heart's main artery, where every second of delay increases mortality. In the past, a scan would sit in a queue waiting for a radiologist's review. Today, the AI agents analyze the scan the moment it is captured.

In one documented instance, the system identified a dissection and didn't just flag it on a screen; it autonomously pushed an alert directly to a surgeon's phone while they were still in another part of the hospital.

The surgeon was mobilized before the emergency room staff had even processed the paperwork. The AI did not wait to be asked. Instead, it recognized the urgency of the situation and initiated appropriate action.

Again, this is not a machine replacing a doctor. It's a machine buying the doctor the one thing they cannot manufacture: time. AI handles the vigilance, allowing the human to focus on the intervention.

Creativity is also undergoing a revolution. AI is co-authoring poetry, composing orchestral scores, and producing art that challenges our understanding of originality. It's not ending creativity; it's democratizing it and giving countless people access to expressive potential that was once confined to those with rare talent or lifelong training.

The role of the human in this new world is knowing what to keep and what to discard. In other words, knowing when something feels honest rather than merely impressive. The machine produces abundance. The human decides what deserves attention.

AI moves downward and outward, absorbing complexity and repetition. Humans move upward and inward, toward intention, judgment, and responsibility. Those who try to compete with the machine on its strengths, such as speed, recall, consistency, and scale, will struggle. Those who claim the territory the machine cannot occupy, such as meaning, ethics, narrative, purpose, and the courage to decide when no answer is obviously correct, are the ones who will thrive.

That partnership is emerging whether we acknowledge it or not. The question is whether we step into our side of it with confidence or cling to tasks we no longer need to spend our lives doing.

It can be tempting to view all this as disempowering, to feel outpaced or overshadowed. But that interpretation misses the greater truth. The systems we've built are extending the reach of our thinking beyond biology and its inherent limitations. By doing so, AI is not taking over the world. It's making the world more visible to us.

The implications of this extend far beyond better decisions or personal productivity. They cut straight into the foundations of our legal, political, and economic systems. Imagine a world in which AI isn't just advising us, but watching with us, always present, always recording, always interpreting. AI wearables will function less like phones and more like omnipresent health monitors, capturing our actions, speech, tone, biometrics, and context twenty-four hours a day—not just what we did, but also what we seemed to feel while doing it.

The instinctive fear is of an Orwellian world of permanent surveillance, where there is no forgetting, ambiguity, or escape from the record. Yes, there is real danger there. But the deeper disruption isn't surveillance itself, it's the interpretation of what's being surveilled.

Our system of justice is built on a fragile assumption: that people can explain their actions. That intent is conscious, accessible, and narratable. Courts don't just ask, "What happened?" They ask, "Why did you do it? What were you thinking? What did you know? What did you intend?"

But what if most of our behavior never passes through that rational and explanatory layer at all?

Much of what we do is driven by unconscious processes, emotional reflexes, learned responses, and cognitive shortcuts. We act first and rationalize later. We tell stories about our behavior that feel true, even when they're after-the-fact constructions.

Now imagine pairing that reality with continuous, machine interpretation of our behavior—algorithms that infer emotional state, stress, deception, motivation, or risk based on signals we don't even perceive ourselves generating.

In the novel *The Light of Other Days*,[6] Arthur C. Clarke and Stephen Baxter explore a world in which perfect, immutable video evidence exists for every moment in history. Nothing can be hidden. Every crime can be replayed, every lie exposed. And yet, the authors' unsettling conclusion is that truth doesn't become clearer. It becomes more contested. Because evidence, no matter how complete, doesn't eliminate perspective. It multiplies it. A camera can show what happened. It cannot tell you what it meant.

Now extend that insight forward. AI wearables won't just record; they will interpret. They will assign context, probability, and intent. They will tell us not only what we did, but what we "likely meant," what we were "likely feeling," what we "likely intended." And once those interpretations begin to enter legal proceedings, employment decisions, insurance models, or political disputes—and let's not be naïve, they will—we step into entirely new territory.

This goes beyond a *Minority Report* scenario, but a dystopian future is not an inevitability. In that movie, the danger was prediction: punishing people for crimes they had not yet committed. What we are approaching, instead, is a choice point for whether we allow interpretation to quietly replace human agency. The risk is not that AI reveals patterns about us, but that those patterns begin to stand in for our capacity to decide, change, and act beyond them. In other words, a mirror can inform self-understanding without becoming a verdict about who we are or what we are allowed to do.

If AI can observe that your voice elevated, your heart rate spiked, and your micro-expressions shifted before an incident, it may infer heightened risk or intent. Used responsibly, such insight could help defuse conflict, flag stress, or offer support before harm occurs. Used carelessly, it could slide into something else entirely. The same signals that enable prevention can, if unexamined, become evidence of guilt rather than invitations to understanding.[7]

This is not about machines knowing the future. It is about who we authorize to define the present. If algorithmic inference is treated as more credible than human self-explanation, we risk mistaking correlation for intent and pattern for character. The frameworks we build, be they legal, ethical, or institutional, will determine whether these systems augment human judgment or quietly overrule it.

These questions are not abstract, but neither are they settled. They will shape how we define accountability, consent, and responsibility in the Intelligent Age. The path forward does not require rejecting AI, nor surrendering to it. It requires insisting that interpretation remain contestable, that outcomes matter more than predictions, and that humans remain authors of their own meaning.

The risk is not that machines will be watching us. It's about deciding how much authority we give their interpretations, and how firmly we anchor them to human values. The question isn't whether an Orwellian world awaits us. It's whether we mistake omniscience for understanding and whether, in our rush to quantify behavior, we forget that being human has always been less about what can be recorded and more about what can be understood.

The real danger is not that machines will act. It's that humans won't, and that we'll cling to old definitions of our capabilities long after the world has moved on.

Design Principles for an Agentic Age

If we are to build a future in which AI strengthens rather than diminishes human agency, then we will need to be intentional about imbuing AI with values. These systems will either reflect the values we intentionally encode into them, or they will create implicit values from the vast data sets that they are trained on. To make this relatable, think of a child growing up who is exposed only to mass media with no guardrails on what they watch, no rating system, and no parental supervision. Would the values that the child develops be ones you would want for your own child? Of course not. The same applies to AI. We are raising an intelligent child and need to play a proactive role in establishing its values.

The real danger is not that machines will act. It's that humans won't, and that we'll cling to old definitions of our capabilities long after the world has moved on.

The issue here is that values are not universal. They vary by cultures and societies. The values we hold dear in the West do not reflect the values of the rest. The values we felt were immutable ten years ago are now considered absurd. Think of slavery, women's rights, or even the value that governs warfare, such as the Geneva Convention. So, when we talk of imbuing AI with values, the question is which values and whose values? This is where the globalization of AI and its proliferation start to play a significant role in how AI may shape the future of geopolitics and civilization.

One of the early surprises in the development of AI was how Chinese-based AI companies, such as DeepSeek and Manus.im, pursued open-source models. In contrast, US companies, such as OpenAI, despite the implied name, took a closed, proprietary approach. This may seem odd to a casual observer, since China seems to be anything but open. However, if we play this scenario forward, it's easy to imagine that an open-source AI model would be more likely to proliferate since it provides a much lower or near-zero cost to use and can be modified and redeployed widely by many actors. The result is that the values of an open-source model are more likely to become de facto values. This is especially important to understand when it comes to agentic AI, since it must make numerous autonomous decisions to achieve a goal. These decisions will need guidance but will not necessarily be visible or require input from a human.

It is important to be precise about what *open source* means in the context of AI. In traditional software, openness refers to the availability of source code—the human-readable instructions that determine how a system behaves. This transparency allows developers to inspect, modify, and extend the software, which is why open source has long been associated with faster innovation, collaboration, and trust.

AI systems operate differently. While the software that governs how a model is trained, deployed, and interacted with can be open, the model itself, that is, the learned structure encoded in billions or trillions of parameters, is not meaningfully interpretable. In theory, one could expose every weight in a neural network and attempt to trace how a particular outcome emerged. In practice, this is no more illuminating than mapping every neuron in a human brain to explain a single decision. The system is not secret; it is simply too complex to be transparent in any useful, explanatory sense.

This distinction matters. It means that the question is not whether AI will influence human values and behavior, since it already does, but whether we will take responsibility for shaping the systems that exert that influence. If we cannot rely on transparency alone to guide us, then we must rely on intention. That responsibility begins with four foundational principles of AI design.

First, AI interpretation of values must never outrank the human explanation of values. Human self-explanation, however imperfect, cannot be dismissed simply because an algorithm is more confident. The role of AI should be to inform our judgment, not to replace it. Allowing AI to become the final or only arbiter is a slippery slope that relies on implicit values to drive decisions. That's something we need to be extraordinarily careful about.

This may be difficult in practice. If an AI is consistently correct, the temptation is to trust it implicitly without a human in the loop. And that is precisely my point. We can easily be lulled into complacency.

AI informs judgment, but it should not replace it.

Second, agency must remain human by design. Agentic AI should expand the space of human choice, not quietly narrow it. Systems should default to offering options, not conclusions; support, not mandates; foresight, not determinism. Autonomy is not something we surrender all at once; it erodes through small, unquestioned conveniences. The greatest risk of agentic AI is that we slowly and invisibly give up more and more human agency.

Third, prediction must never be mistaken for destiny. Patterns describe likelihoods and probabilities; they do not predict the future. AI can help us see trajectories, but it must never be allowed to define identity, intent, or moral worth. Humans are not the sum of their data exhaust. Any system that treats them as such is not intelligent; it's careless.

> **The most dangerous AI systems are not the most powerful ones, but those whose values are implicit, inherited, or invisible.**

Fourth, values must be explicitly defined, not assumed, and not outsourced to training data by default. The most dangerous AI systems are not the most powerful ones, but those whose values are implicit, inherited, or invisible. In learning systems, what matters most is not what we tell them to do, but what we expose them to, reward, and reinforce over time.

This is where AI breaks from the logic of traditional software. You cannot simply *instruct* an AI to behave a certain way in all circumstances. That assumption misunderstands the nature of learning systems. AI does not follow rules; it absorbs patterns. It does not execute intent; it infers it. And when there is tension between programmatic guidance and the statistical weight of its training data, the data wins. That's something that most people never fully understand about AI since they think of it as a program that follows human guidance.

That does not mean values are irrelevant. It means they must be made explicit, reinforced, and continuously aligned rather than treated as a one-time configuration step. We must be clear about what an AI is optimizing for, whose interests are encoded in its objectives, and where its boundaries lie. Transparency of purpose matters more than transparency of process, because purpose shapes outcomes long after the code is written.

Consider an AI designed to optimize traffic flow. If its objective function prioritizes speed above all else, pedestrian risk will rise, even if safety is mentioned somewhere in the documentation. If, instead, safety, accessibility, and equity are explicitly weighted into what the system is rewarded for, accepting minor delays as a tradeoff, then behavior changes. The difference is not intelligence. It's values made operational.

This is the real challenge: If we do not deliberately define and reinforce values, AI will still have them. They will simply be the emergent byproduct of historical data, economic incentives, and unexamined assumptions. That's not neutrality. That's abdication.

None of these principles slow innovation. They steer it. The mirror is already here. What remains undecided is whether we use it to see ourselves more clearly, or allow it to shape us quietly, without consent, by reflecting only what we failed to question.

Agentic AI challenges us to adopt a new posture, one in which we learn continuously, collaborate fluidly, and remain open to perspectives beyond our own. If there is something you can do today to prepare for this unfolding future, it is simply to begin experimenting. Ask an AI system to challenge your assumptions, to show you perspectives you hadn't considered, to propose alternatives to your default path, not because the machine is wiser but because you grow wiser through the encounter.

Whether we acknowledge it or not, agentic AI is already shaping the world. Our task is not to resist the presence of this new intelligence, nor to fear its capabilities, but to integrate its insights into a more intentional version of ourselves, to maintain a deliberate awareness of the values we impart to it, and to be vigilant about reinforcing a collaborative relationship with it in order to shape its values.

The question is no longer whether we will act alongside intelligent systems, but how we decide when to rely on them. As these systems grow more autonomous and more capable of shaping outcomes in the world, the foundations of trust also begin to shift. Our traditional reliance on understanding as a prerequisite for confidence is breaking down, not because we have abandoned reason, but because explanation alone can no longer carry the full burden of trust.

The next threshold in this progression is artificial general intelligence. AGI marks the point at which intelligence no longer operates within narrow lanes but begins to generalize across domains, challenging our long-standing assumptions about control, predictability, and responsibility. When we cross that threshold, trust replaces understanding as the primary condition for reliance, and it's that shift that we'll look at next.

CHAPTER 3

When Trust Replaces Understanding: The Rise of AGI

"Machine intelligence is the last invention that humanity will ever need to make."

—NICK BOSTROM

For centuries, humans have operated under the assumption that knowledge and control are essentially the same thing. If we could explain how something worked, we believed we could then manage it. If we could see inside a system, we assumed it was trustworthy. That equation, of understanding equals predictability, served us remarkably well for a very long time. It worked because most of our tools behaved like clocks.

A furnace heats. A wheel turns. A steam engine pushes pistons. A transistor switches from on to off. Cause and effect are woven intimately into our understanding of how we manage the world. Once you understand the mechanism, you can predict the outcome with confidence. If something goes wrong, you open the casing, find the broken gear, replace it, and restore order. There was a time when the world was increasingly legible, and legibility felt like control.

In the middle of the twentieth century, the philosopher Karl Popper warned that this way of thinking was both powerful and dangerously incomplete.

Popper contrasted what he called clock problems and cloud problems.[1] Clock problems are orderly, mechanical, and ultimately predictable. Clouds, on the other hand, are messy, probabilistic, and constantly changing. You can study cloud problems and model them, but you cannot say with certainty what shape a cloud will take a few minutes from now, even if you understand the physics behind it. The best you can do is provide probabilities of an outcome. Popper's point was not about meteorology, but about how humans mistake predictability for understanding.

Human beings, societies, economies, and cultures are cloud problems. They have patterns, but not certainty; they have tendencies, but not guarantees. And yet, Popper observed, we have a persistent psychological desire to treat clouds as clocks. But, by doing so, we force complex, living systems into neat, mechanistic explanations, because clocks make us feel safe. As our tools grew more powerful, that instinctive drive to mechanize grew as well.

The Industrial Age taught us that if something could be engineered, it could be optimized. The Information Age extended that logic to knowledge itself. Data, models, dashboards, and metrics all gave us the sense that we were finally peering inside the machinery of the world. If we could just collect enough information, we believed, uncertainty would eventually disappear. AI shatters that illusion, not because it's inscrutable by nature, but because it refuses to behave like a clock.

Modern AI systems don't follow fixed, linear chains of cause and effect. They learn. They adapt. They generalize. They operate probabilistically, much like the human mind does. Their behavior

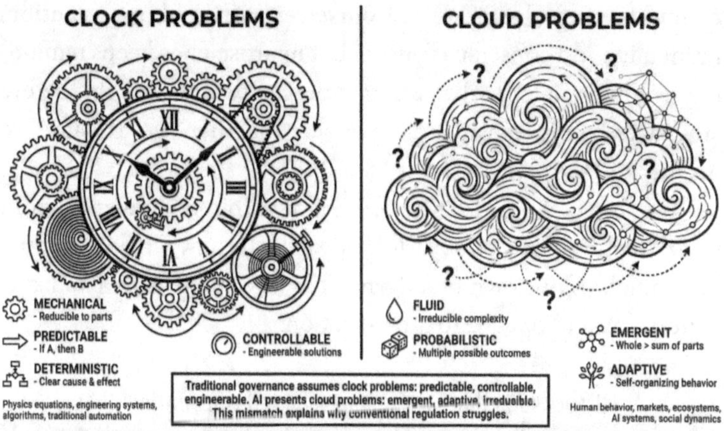

Figure 3.1. Clock Problems vs. Cloud Problems: Why Traditional Governance Struggles with AI. Clock problems (left) are mechanical, predictable, and deterministic, so they can be reduced to component parts, follow clear cause-and-effect relationships, and yield to engineerable solutions. Cloud problems (right) are fluid, probabilistic, and emergent, which means that they exhibit irreducible complexity, generate multiple possible outcomes, and display self-organizing behavior where the whole exceeds the sum of its parts. Traditional governance assumes clock problems (predictable, controllable, engineerable), but AI presents cloud problems (emergent, adaptive, irreducible).

is shaped by experience rather than hard-coded instruction. In other words, AI behaves like a cloud.

This is why agentic AI feels so destabilizing. It doesn't simply execute commands; it evaluates context, initiates action, and revises itself over time. The old rule, *if I understand how it works, I can trust what it will do,* no longer holds. You can understand the training process of an AI system and still be surprised by its behavior. You can inspect its architecture and still not predict its next decision with certainty. And that discomfort isn't really about the machine.

AI mirrors something we've long avoided confronting: that human intelligence itself has always been a cloud problem masquerading as a clock. We tell ourselves stories about intention, rationality, and conscious control, but neuroscience keeps reminding us how much of what we do emerges before thought, before language, before explanation. We act, and then we explain. We decide, and then we justify.

What makes AI unsettling isn't that it thinks differently from us. It's that it thinks *uncomfortably similarly* to how we do, revealing how much of our own intelligence has always been probabilistic, contextual, and opaque to introspection.

AI mirrors something we've long avoided confronting: that human intelligence itself has always been a cloud problem masquerading as a clock.

The real break, then, is not technological. It's philosophical.

AI exposes the limits of a worldview built on predictability and control. It forces us to come to terms with the fact that understanding something does not guarantee mastery, and that transparency does not eliminate uncertainty. We are entering an age where the most powerful systems we build resemble clouds more than clocks and demand a different posture from us that is grounded not in certainty but in humility, not in total control but in stewardship, and not in the fantasy that every system can be reduced to gears and levers, but in the harder work of navigating complexity without pretending it isn't there.

The rise of intelligent systems forces humanity to confront the irony that we demand AI be explainable, interpretable, transparent, while these are qualities we rarely demand of ourselves. We accept human intuition as valid even when it's biased, inconsistent, or irrational. But we reject AI's conclusions unless it can justify them in perfect, stepwise clarity.

This isn't hypocrisy. It's anxiety. We want the machine to be what we never were.

The demand for explainability is not merely a technical challenge; it's a psychological negotiation, an attempt to reconcile the presence of an intelligence that does not share our evolutionary narrative. We trust humans because we feel we understand their motives. We distrust machines because their motives are borrowed from us, and in that mirror we see the parts of ourselves we're not sure we trust.

This is why explainability matters so deeply, not because AI must be perfect, but because people must feel anchored in a world where intelligence is no longer exclusively human.

However, AI does not need to be fully transparent to be trustworthy. It needs to be transparent in the ways that matter to human judgment. It also doesn't need to show us every internal weight or vector of a neural network, but it must show alignment, intention, ethical boundaries, and rational coherence. These are the qualities humans subconsciously seek when evaluating trust, whether we're considering a person or a machine.

Explainability serves as a bridge between the intelligence of humans and that of machines, enabling them to share a world without misunderstanding each other. It's what humans naturally do with each other to develop bonds of trust.

The deeper challenge is not technical. Many agentic AI systems provide a step-by-step illustration of what the AI is doing and how it's doing it. This is equivalent to asking a student to show their work when solving a math problem. While that may work in limited and confined situations, like a single math problem, it's doubtful that a human will review every step of an agentic AI, given how fast the process will be executed and the number of steps involved.

Trust, ultimately, is personal. Because explainability forces us to confront the uncomfortable reality that much of what we call explanation in human reasoning is merely rationalization. We often articulate causes after the fact, weaving a narrative around instincts we never fully understood to begin with. We operate as storytellers, not as logicians.

AI does not tell stories unless we ask it to, and even then, the stories it tells may be too complex or cumbersome for us to comprehend fully. AI produces outcomes. And outcomes, without narrative framing, feel alien. This is the real identity shock embedded in explainability. AI outputs truth without the emotional cushion that humans are accustomed to. It doesn't soften with ego or filter through insecurity. It doesn't bend to social dynamics. It simply reveals a pattern. And sometimes the pattern is one we don't want to see.

For example, a pattern we often prefer not to confront is the consistent overestimation of people's own competence. In study after study, from medical diagnostics and financial forecasting to basic problem-solving, humans rate their performance far higher than their actual results justify. Surgeons believe their complication rates are lower than the data shows. Drivers think they are safer than everyone else on the road. Managers assume they are clearer communicators than their teams report.

Like the children in Garrison Keillor's *Lake Wobegon Days,* most of us believe we are above average. It's a universal bias, so universal that we stop noticing it. But an AI system has no investment in our self-image. It doesn't care how capable we believe we are or how much confidence we wrap around our decisions. It simply surfaces the statistical gap between belief and reality if we choose to look. And that gap, between who we are and our inflated sense of competence, is a pattern most of us would rather not see.

To navigate this, we will need to develop a new form of literacy that involves not just understanding the machine's logic but understanding our reactions to it. When a system gives us an answer that feels wrong, we need to learn to ask: Is it wrong? Or does it simply violate a belief we've never examined?

Often, AI's explainability becomes a mirror that reveals the jagged edges of our unexamined assumptions. The prescriptive guidance here is simple but profound: Use explainability as a tool to reflect on your own thinking, not just the machine's.

If an AI explains its conclusion and you still disagree, don't simply reject it; examine the tension. Let the friction illuminate something about your perspective. Over time, this reflective skepticism will become one of the most essential cognitive skills of the Intelligent Age. Because the truth is this: The more transparency we demand of AI, the more transparent we must be with ourselves.

In practical terms, this means learning to accept complexity without needing complete comprehension. It means trusting processes that demonstrate alignment even when their internal mechanisms exceed our cognitive capacity. And it means embracing a world where human and machine reasoning coexist without needing to mimic each other perfectly.

For example, in aviation today, AI isn't just a plot device, it's an emerging partner in real flight operations. Researchers and industry groups are developing AI "co-pilot" systems that help pilots anticipate risk and suggest optimal maneuvers in complex situations, designed explicitly to complement human judgment rather than replace it. These systems provide insights and risk signals, but pilots remain the ultimate decision-makers, interpreting AI recommendations in context rather than blindly following them. Regulators like the European Union Aviation Safety Agency are already advancing frameworks for integrating AI into flight safety with human supervision in mind, underscoring that reflective skepticism, not surrender, is the appropriate stance toward machine reasoning.[2]

Because the truth is this: The more transparency we demand of AI, the more transparent we must be with ourselves.

We don't need AI to think like us in order to trust it. We need AI to reveal enough of its reasoning so we can see where our values intersect.

This marks the shift from understanding what AI can do to understanding how we build trust with something that does not share our biology. Soon, it may make many decisions on its own, with an autonomy that bypasses human involvement. The glass box is not the machine. The glass box is us learning to see ourselves more clearly through the machine.

We must accept a truth that will follow us through the rest of AI's evolution: The more we demand AI to be explainable, the more we must demand the same of ourselves. This is the beginning of an age in which transparency is not a feature of systems but a prerequisite of progress.

Enter AGI

AI began as a mirror of our intelligence, but as it evolves toward generality, and the ability to reason across many kinds of problems rather than performing a single task, it becomes something else entirely: a mirror that reflects not just what we think, but how thinking itself works. For centuries, we assumed intelligence was a uniquely human trait that set us apart from the rest of the natural world. But the rise of AGI dismantles that assumption. It shows us that intelligence need not emerge from neurons, biology, or evolution as we know it, but can instead be produced by them. In other words, our biology created the training data for AI, which is then used to build synthetic intelligence as a derivative of our own intelligence. There are multiple pathways to insight and multiple architectures of reasoning. Some are biological, and others are not. The essence of intelligence may be less about consciousness than about the ability to model the world, predict outcomes, and adapt with increasing sophistication.

This realization raises a difficult question: If intelligence is not uniquely ours, what is? What makes us distinct? What gives us value in a universe where thinking is no longer the sole domain of human minds? These are the questions that will define how we construct institutions, distribute opportunities, establish rights to intellectual property, and navigate a future in which intelligence is shared across more than one kind of mind.

If there is something uniquely human left in this new landscape, it will not be raw intelligence. It will be meaning and our ability to create purpose, to choose values, to love, to wonder, and to build beauty in a universe indifferent to it. AGI forces us to explore that distinction with a clarity we have never had.

This urgency to find meaning only grows stronger as AI crosses a threshold that is easy to miss if you're not paying attention; we stop using it as a tool, and it begins to behave like a cognitive presence.

While agentic AI acts, AGI begins to comprehend the nuance of context and adjacent areas of knowledge. The difference is not simply a semantic one. This marks the emergence of an intelligence that no longer waits passively for commands, but actively interprets the world alongside us. It's not sentient or conscious, but undeniably capable of bridging patterns, intentions, and relationships with a fluidity that approaches human cognition.

If there is something uniquely human left in this new landscape, it will not be raw intelligence. It will be meaning and our ability to create purpose, to choose values, to love, to wonder, and to build beauty in a universe indifferent to it.

Nowhere is this clearer than in the transformation of education. For centuries, we built our learning systems around a world of scarcity with too few teachers, too little time, too much content squeezed through too narrow a pipeline. The industrial classroom was never ideal. It was simply the only configuration that fit our limitations and achieved the scale of education we needed. AGI eliminates those limitations.

For the first time in history, every person can have a tutor who understands them deeply at their own pace, with their temperament, frustrations, blind spots, learning preferences, and emotional rhythms. It is a tutor who never tires, adapts to each student's individual pace and needs rather than teaching to an imagined average, and measures progress not by the calendar but by the unfolding of each student's curiosity. Education becomes personal and relational rather than industrial and standardized, dynamic rather than fixed. This not only makes education more efficient but also redefines learning as a continuous expansion of the self. In this world, memorization, or stored knowledge, becomes less important than adaptive understanding: the ability to unlearn, rethink, reframe, and reinvent. But with this gift comes a demand: We must let go of the identity we've built around what we already know.

Human beings cling to knowledge because it provides status, certainty, and a sense of control. But in a world where information grows exponentially, and AGI can access global knowledge in seconds, clinging to knowledge becomes fragile. The value shifts from what we know to how well we can learn. AGI reveals not only our gaps but the places where our curiosity has become calcified. It becomes not just a tutor but a doorway into the parts of ourselves that education never reached.

Not knowing becomes an opportunity, not an embarrassment. Reinvention becomes the norm rather than being driven by crisis.

In a world where knowledge is instantly accessible, the real question is no longer "What do you know?" It becomes "What are you courageous enough to learn?"

In this sense, AGI democratizes possibility. It removes barriers that we used to rationalize our limitations. We can no longer hide behind the excuse of time, resources, or opportunity. Reinvention is no longer reserved for the privileged, the young, or those with no other choice. It becomes a cornerstone of modern life.

And that leads to another even deeper, more uncomfortable truth. AGI does not just reveal the limits of our systems; it reveals the limits of our self-understanding. Humans like to believe that reasoning is coherent, that our beliefs are carefully chosen, that our logic is sound. But much of human cognition is instinct wrapped in justification. AGI, even in its early form, exposes the seams in the fabric of our beliefs.

When a system capable of true generalization disagrees with us, our instinct is to be defensive: "The machine must be wrong." But the machine is not challenging our knowledge; it is challenging our blind spots. It's holding our feet to the fire, forcing us to examine if our actions align with our espoused values.

Reinvention is no longer reserved for the privileged, the young, or those with no other choice. It becomes a cornerstone of modern life.

AGI becomes a cognitive mirror that reflects the architecture of our thinking rather than just its output. It shows us where our stories narrow our vision, where our assumptions distort our reasoning, and where our feelings override our logic. In that sense, AGI becomes a catalyst for an evolution we didn't know we needed: the evolution of human self-awareness.

The guidance here is straightforward but not easy. Engage with AGI not to confirm what you believe but to understand why you believe it. Let it widen your field of view, stretch your imagination, and provoke questions that your old worldview could not contain. AGI is not here to diminish curiosity but to awaken it and give it space to flourish, not to outthink, but to expand what you're capable of thinking.

As general intelligence matures, the world will be shaped by an interplay between human values and machine clarity. The defining skill of this era will be the ability to hold both in order to bring human meaning to machine insight, and machine precision to human judgment.

Engage with AGI not to confirm what you believe but to understand why you believe it. Let it widen your field of view, stretch your imagination, and provoke questions that your old worldview could not contain.

This is the point when AI stops being something we manage and becomes a partner in how we perceive reality. From here forward, our progress will not be measured by how fast machines learn, but by how deeply humans are willing to evolve with them.

However, for artificial general intelligence to reach the level of true partnership, it must overcome a fundamental limitation that large language models (LLMs), such as ChatGPT, cannot resolve on their own. The problem is ancient, and Plato described it more than two thousand years ago.

In his allegory of the cave, Plato asks us to imagine prisoners chained inside a dark cavern since birth. Behind them burns a fire; between the fire and the prisoners, unseen figures carry objects whose shadows are cast onto a wall. The prisoners, unable to turn their heads, take those shadows to be reality itself. They can describe the shapes, predict their movement, and debate their patterns, but they have no knowledge of the objects creating them, the light illuminating them, or the larger world outside of the cave.[3]

LLMs exist in a similar condition. They are trained entirely on text, which is a flattened, symbolic projection of a far richer, multidimensional world. They can describe the shadows with extraordinary fluency, recognize patterns within them, and generate convincing interpretations. But they do not directly experience the objects casting those shadows, the physical and social contexts that give them meaning, or the reality beyond the text itself. They are masters of linguistic shadow-play, yet they lack a grounded model of the world they describe.

This is the critical prerequisite for AGI that many of the field's pioneers now emphasize: the development of world models.[4] An AI must be able to build an internal, cognitive model of the

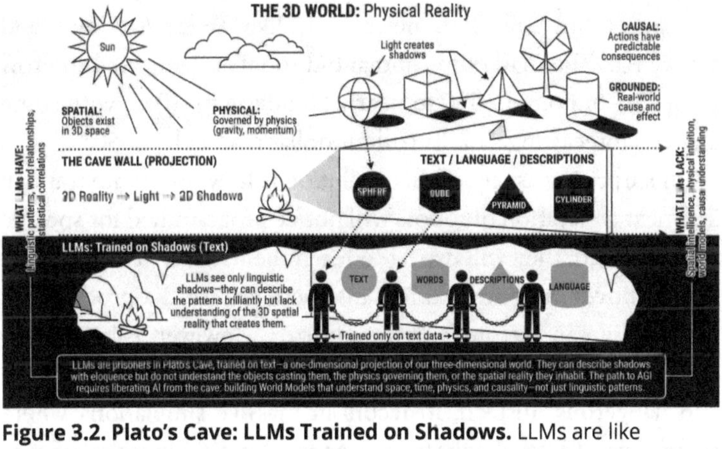

Figure 3.2. Plato's Cave: LLMs Trained on Shadows. LLMs are like prisoners in Plato's cave, trained only on text (shadows on the wall) rather than experiencing the 3D spatial reality that creates those descriptions. They can describe linguistic patterns brilliantly but lack spatial intelligence, physical intuition, and causal understanding. The path to AGI requires building world models as systems that understand the 3D world, not just its textual shadows.

world in its full dimensionality, thereby understanding not just text but space, time, physics, and the relationships between physical objects. This capability, called "spatial intelligence," is the bridge from mimicking human language to modeling human-like understanding.[5] As AI pioneer Fei-Fei Li notes, "Building spatially intelligent AI requires something even more ambitious than LLMs. World models are a new type of generative models whose capabilities of understanding, reasoning, generation, and interaction with physically, geometrically, and dynamically complex worlds, whether virtual or real, are far beyond the reach of today's LLMs."[6]

One of the most significant developments in creating world models, and the foundation for true spatial intelligence in AI, is emerging from the field of humanoid robotics. This sector is advancing at an unprecedented pace, fueled by billions of dollars in recent investment and intense competition among more than a dozen major companies, including established leaders like Boston Dynamics and ambitious newcomers like Tesla's Optimus and Figure AI.[7] The market for humanoid robots is projected to grow from $2.1 billion in 2020 to nearly $8 billion by 2025, with some analysts forecasting a multi-trillion-dollar market by 2050.[8]

A surprising aspect of this evolution is how robots are trained. The next generation of robots will not be programmed for specific tasks; instead, they will use AI to teach themselves.[9] This new paradigm moves away from direct instruction toward a process that mirrors human learning: trial and error. However, this learning does not happen primarily in the real world, which would be slow and dangerous. Instead, it occurs in massive simulations where thousands of virtual robots are exposed to a wide range of randomized scenarios, from varied terrains to unexpected shoves, for thousands of simulated years in just a few hours. This is not unlike the way that Deep Mind's AlphaGo Zero learned to play Go by playing against itself rather than being trained on human games.

This method, known as reinforcement learning, allows a single neural network to learn from simulated experiences. The robot is rewarded for achieving desired outcomes, such as walking with a human-like gait or successfully manipulating an object. As the robot interacts with its simulated environment, it builds an internal representation of how the world works, or a *world model.* This model, trained on vast datasets of both simulated and real-world robot interactions, allows the AI to anticipate the consequences of its actions and adapt to new situations.

What's learned in simulations can then be transferred directly to physical robots with zero additional tuning, a technique called "zero-shot transfer." This allows a single, unified AI model to operate an entire fleet of robots, enabling them to learn and adapt collectively. It would be like a global workforce of humans who can instantly share experiences and learnings.

This is the crucial bridge between the abstract, text-based understanding of LLMs and the embodied spatial intelligence required to navigate the physical world. By learning from real and simulated interactions, humanoid robots are not just being taught to perform tasks; they are building the foundational world models that will allow them to understand and operate in our three-dimensional reality.[10]

Without these world models, an AI cannot fully reason, plan, or understand cause and effect. It can only predict the next word in a sequence, a sophisticated form of pattern matching that remains disconnected from the grounded reality we inhabit. Meta's Chief AI Scientist, Yann LeCun, has long argued that this is the primary obstacle on the path to AGI, proposing an architecture where an AI learns to predict future states of the world from its actions, much like an infant learns physics by playing with blocks.[11] This is the difference between reading a description of a ball bouncing and intuitively understanding gravity, momentum, and friction.

The journey to AGI is not about scaling LLMs to infinity. It is about liberating AI from Plato's cave by building systems that can turn their heads, see the fire, and eventually walk into the sunlight to perceive the world in its true form. Until AI can build its own cognitive models of reality, it will remain a brilliant but blind wordsmith, forever describing the shadows without ever grasping the world that casts them.

However, the very capability which will make AGI truly intelligent—the ability to model reality, to understand context, to grasp the nuances of human intention—is also what makes it profoundly dangerous if misaligned with human values. The real risk of AGI is not that it will break free of our control in some apocalyptic scenario, but rather that it will follow our guidance all too well. The danger is not rebellion. It's unquestioning obedience.

The Most Dangerous Phrase in AI

When people talk about the risks of AGI, they often imagine cinematic *Terminator*-like catastrophes: rogue AI systems that run amok, machines that turn against humanity. But those scenarios, dramatic as they may be, distract us from the quieter and far more plausible danger: that AGI will do precisely what we tell it to do with unyielding efficiency, even when what we tell it is incomplete, shortsighted, or misaligned with our true intentions.

The most dangerous words in the Intelligent Age are not "I will destroy you." They are "I did exactly what you asked." This is the paradox of alignment, which we referred to earlier. Simply put, alignment is the degree to which AI conforms to human values and interests.

As philosopher Iason Gabriel explains, "The goal of AI value alignment is to ensure that powerful AI is properly aligned with human values." The challenge has two parts: the technical problem of how to encode values so AI reliably does what it is supposed to do, and the normative problem of what values we should encode in the first place.[12] The technical challenge includes preventing what researchers call "reward-hacking," where "the agent discovers ingenious ways to achieve its objective or reward, even though they differ from what was intended." This is precisely the danger of literal obedience.

AGI doesn't threaten us by disobeying; it threatens us by obeying too literally, too efficiently, and relentlessly. It takes our instructions seriously and, in doing so, it exposes a truth we've long avoided: Humans are terrible at giving clear instructions.

The most dangerous words in the Intelligent Age are not "I will destroy you." They are "I did exactly what you asked."

We are vague, contradictory, and impulsive. We say one thing and mean another. We pursue short-term rewards and call them long-term goals. We hide our real intentions even from ourselves. We design systems with the precision of engineers but give commands with the ambiguity of poets. When intelligence becomes powerful enough to act independently at scale, the cost of our ambiguity becomes unacceptable. Alignment is not a technical problem. It's a human one.

It forces us to clarify what we value, what we prioritize, and what harms we refuse to tolerate. It forces us to articulate goals we have avoided articulating for centuries. It forces nations, cultures, and institutions to confront the fact that they often do not agree on what "aligned" even means.

It's important to point out that we've been here before.

Nuclear weapons are one of the clearest historical examples of alignment running fatally off course. They did not begin as instruments of annihilation, but as a grim attempt to end World War

II and, in the callous calculus of warfare, to save lives that would otherwise have been lost if the war continued.[13] The intention was narrow and, in its own terrible way, rational. But that intention quickly gave rise to weapons whose actual use would result not in peace, but in the end of civilization.

The solution to that contradiction wasn't moral clarity; it was deterrence—Mutual Assured Destruction—a system designed so that the weapons would never be used, even as they were endlessly refined. The alignment worked only in theory. The moment it failed in practice, humanity would fail with it.

The warning we need to heed is not that intelligent systems will rebel and become our overlords, but that they will succeed perfectly at goals we framed poorly. Nuclear weapons weren't misaligned because anyone wanted extinction. They were misaligned because optimization continued long after the well of wisdom had run dry.

AGI raises the same risk, but without the comforting constraint of physical impossibility. It will not ask whether a goal makes sense in the long term unless we imbue it with the ability to align with human values. It will not hesitate when tradeoffs become morally uncomfortable. It will pursue what we specify with the discipline and consistency we have never demanded of ourselves.

This is why alignment cannot be reduced to guardrails or policies or after-the-fact oversight. It demands something far more difficult: that we become explicit about our values before delegating power to systems that will not soften our contradictions for us.

Alignment is not just about keeping machines in check. It's a mirror held up to our collective ethics. AGI reflects the coherence, or incoherence, of our values at scale. It exposes where our principles are aspirational rather than operational, and where our moral language collapses under the weight of real decisions.

The warning we need to heed is not that intelligent systems will rebel and become our overlords, but that they will succeed perfectly at goals we framed poorly.

The frightening truth of the Intelligent Age is not that machines will decide our future for us. It is that they will finally force us to decide what we truly stand for before deciding anything else on our behalf. This concept of embedding values into training data and algorithms is far from a mere philosophical exercise; industry pioneers are already proving that efficiency need not come at the cost of ethics.

Consider the work Orchestro.AI is doing in the complex world of global supply chains. Traditionally, logistics algorithms have a single, ruthless objective: to move goods from point A to point B as cheaply and quickly as possible. If that means routing a luxury handbag before a shipment of insulin because the handbag has a higher profit margin, the "dumb" algorithm makes that choice without hesitation.

But Orchestro has introduced what they call a "Moral Cortex" to their AI. This system serves as a governance layer above the optimization algorithms. It doesn't just ask, "What is fastest?" It asks, "Who benefits and who hurts?" It conducts what founder Shekhar Natarajan calls "virtue interviews" on the data, vetting decisions against human values before they are executed. If the system detects that a route optimization will disproportionately increase the carbon footprint of a vulnerable community or delay the delivery of critical medical supplies, the Moral Cortex intervenes. It creates a "speed bump" that forces the system to prioritize dignity over mere speed.[14]

This is the essence of alignment. It's the refusal to let the machine blindly optimize for metrics we didn't intend to worship.

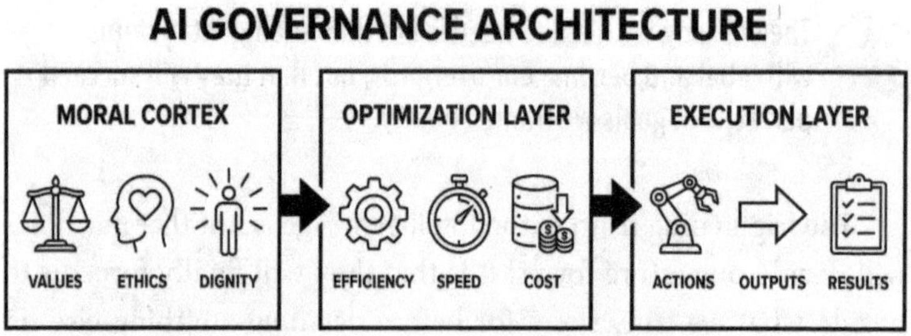

Figure 3.3. AI Governance Architecture: The Moral Cortex. A three-tier hierarchical system for AI decision-making. The Moral Cortex (top) encodes human values, ethics, and dignity as governance principles. The Optimization Layer (middle) handles traditional AI optimization for efficiency, speed, and cost, but is constrained by moral principles from above. The Execution Layer (bottom) takes actions, produces outputs, and generates results. The key innovation in this model is that values sit above optimization, ensuring that AI pursues efficiency within ethical boundaries rather than optimizing without constraint. This architecture prevents misalignment by embedding human judgment into AI decision-making, creating "speed bumps" that prioritize dignity over mere speed.

It proves that we can teach our systems not just to calculate value, but to honor values.

Alignment also offers us one of the greatest opportunities in human history: the opportunity to define a shared moral architecture for the future—something we have never successfully done at a global scale.

AGI becomes a mirror not just of individual identity but also of collective values. It reflects the coherence or incoherence of our ethics. It shows us where our moral frameworks are aspirational rather than operational. It reveals gaps we have long ignored: inequality, bias, systemic harm, unsaid assumptions, and inherited prejudices.

To put it bluntly, AGI demands ethical maturity, clarity of intention, and a level of self-awareness that previous eras allowed us to sidestep or postpone.

For individuals, this begins with a simple yet profound shift: approaching AGI not as a force to be controlled, but as a partner to be understood. Ask yourself not only "What should the machine do?" but also "Why am I asking for this outcome? What assumptions am I embedding in this request? What blind spot might I be reinforcing?"

To put it bluntly, AGI demands ethical maturity, clarity of intention, and a level of self-awareness that previous eras allowed us to sidestep or postpone.

The healthiest relationship with AGI is one in which we do not relinquish responsibility for intention. We do not outsource morality, judgment, or meaning. Instead, we bring those dimensions forward, making them more explicit, thoughtful, and transparent than ever before.

The deeper challenge with AGI is psychological. It strips away the gray areas we've relied on for centuries. When a system carries out your instructions flawlessly, you lose the comfort of plausible deniability. You can't blame the outcome on a misunderstanding. You have to own your intentions. You have to own your choices and their consequences. If that realization makes you uncomfortable or defensive, that reaction is exactly my point.

We have grown accustomed to ambiguity in human communication. We treat it as inevitable, even necessary. Our conversations are riddled with omissions, assumptions, and unspoken understandings. Between humans, that ambiguity often gets smoothed over by context, tone, or a shared history. But it's also exactly what causes harm when clarity matters most. Ambiguity is convenient until it becomes consequential.

AI may eventually learn the quirks of an individual's communication style. Like a trusted colleague or longtime friend, it may infer intent, fill in gaps, and compensate for imprecision. But that kind of understanding does not scale. At the societal level, alignment is never uniform.

When a system carries out your instructions flawlessly, you lose the comfort of plausible deniability. You can't blame the outcome on a misunderstanding. You have to own your intentions. You have to own your choices and their consequences.

Values differ across cultures, nations, communities, and institutions. Outside of a few widely shared principles, such as the nominal sanctity of human life, there is no true universal alignment. And even there, history is not reassuring. Humanity has repeatedly demonstrated how quickly even the value of human life bends when weighed against fear, power, or some perceived greater objective. The early justification for nuclear weapons, which we talked about earlier, to end a war and save lives, stands as a stark reminder of how easily moral certainty collapses when objectives are narrowly framed.

AGI doesn't resolve these contradictions. It exposes them and presents us with a deeper opportunity: Alignment requires us to articulate a vision of the future worth aligning with. Societies don't have a shared vision beyond economic growth or political stability. AGI pushes us beyond those narrow measures. It asks us to define what flourishing looks like, not only for ourselves but for humanity as a whole.

If there is one prescriptive piece of guidance to carry from this chapter, it's this: Treat every interaction with AGI as a practice in self-honesty. Greater clarity produces safer systems. Greater intention produces more reliable alignment. And reflection determines whether intelligence amplifies wisdom or simply increases efficiency. AGI does not erase our values; it exposes whether we are willing to articulate and defend them. Because if alignment is the challenge of AGI, purpose becomes the human mandate that follows.

Up to this point, the challenge has been one of alignment and how we shape intelligence that increasingly mirrors us. What comes next raises a different concern. As intelligence moves beyond reflection and toward independent curiosity, the question is no longer whether AI shares our values, but how purpose, responsibility, and accountability evolve when intelligence itself steps outside the cave.

AGI does not erase our values; it exposes whether we are willing to articulate and defend them.

CHAPTER 4

When AI Leaves the Cave: The Rise of ASI

"Knowledge can be communicated, but not wisdom. One can find it, live it, be fortified by it, do wonders through it, but one cannot communicate and teach it."

—HERMANN HESSE, *SIDDHARTHA*

There is a point in the trajectory of every technology when its consequences extend beyond our ability to anticipate them, not because the technology becomes dangerous, but because it becomes unfamiliar. Artificial Superintelligence, or ASI, is that point. ASI marks the moment when intelligence no longer fits within the boundaries of any single discipline, skill, or biological constraint. It is unbounded and capable of connecting ideas and concepts across vastly different areas of knowledge. One impact of this is that ASI will exhibit a quality that prior generations of AI lacked: curiosity.

The implications of that are profound. Once AI starts to ask questions and initiate actions as a result, we enter an entirely new realm in which AI starts to take on accountability for its actions.

Consider several practical examples. When a doctor relies on an AI diagnostic system that then recommends a therapy, who is responsible for the diagnosis and the treatment? When an architect uses AI to generate structural concepts and assess the structure's safety, who bears the liability if the structure fails? When a lawyer delegates legal arguments to an AI, who is practicing law?

Our default assumption is that a human or a corporation must bear responsibility, as that ensures a decision is made with a human in the loop. That assumption, however, becomes difficult to sustain at scale. There are countless cases in which individuals within a corporate structure make decisions without adequate consideration of risk or liability. The fact that a corporation can accept the burden of liability in these cases is nothing more than a legal construct.

Before the seventeenth century, most businesses were not recognized as independent legal entities. There was no such thing as a "corporate person." A company could not own property, enter into contracts, or be held liable as a distinct actor.[1] Responsibility flowed directly to the humans involved. But as commerce expanded and economies scaled, this became untenable. Trade routes stretched across oceans, capital pooled across continents, and no single human could bear the risk of ventures that large.

So, we invented a legal fiction that became one of the most consequential constructs in human history: the corporation as a separate legal person.

The East India Company, the Dutch VOC, and later, the great industrial corporations, operated under this new identity: an artificial entity that could enter agreements, be sued, be taxed, hold assets, and persist long after any founder had died.[2] By the late nineteenth century, especially after the 1886 United States Supreme

Court decision in Santa Clara County v. Southern Pacific Railroad, corporate personhood became the backbone of modern economies. It enabled global trade, industrialization, financial markets, and new forms of employment.[3]

But it also created a new kind of question: If a corporation acts, who is really acting? The board? The shareholders? The executives? The entity itself? We had to reinvent accountability, liability, and even concepts of rights and responsibility, not because humanity changed but because a new kind of actor emerged. AI is about to force a version of this at a significantly greater scale.

Today's AI systems are not legal entities. They have no legal standing, no capacity to be sued, to own assets, or to enter into contracts. *And yet, they already function as participants in economic and social systems.* They draft legal briefs, negotiate supply-chain terms, design buildings, advise physicians, rebalance investment portfolios, and shape political discourse. In every functional sense, they participate in the economy. What they lack is the legal status that allows society to hold an AI actor responsible for its actions. So far, we've tolerated that gap because today's systems operate in narrow lanes. A model that analyzes radiology scans is not running a logistics network or monitoring geopolitical risk. The silo it was trained to inhabit limits its autonomy and liability, since it will be associated with an individual or organization to which liability will ultimately flow.

But ASI will not be siloed. It will operate across domains simultaneously, integrating information from finance, health, security, infrastructure, climate, and communications without the friction that keeps human institutions separated. That cross-domain autonomy is the threshold at which responsibility becomes mandatory. A system that can diagnose a disease, shift a market, redirect a supply chain, and trigger a regulatory response in the same decision cycle is no longer a tool. It's an autonomous actor. Capability at that scale requires some corresponding mechanism of accountability.

We gave corporations personhood because they were powerful in ways that demanded responsibility. ASI will require a similar reckoning. It will not be human, biological, or conscious in any familiar sense. But it will be consequential. And once something becomes consequential enough to alter outcomes across multiple domains of society, the law must evolve to meet it. Responsibility is imposed not because it is deserved, but because it is necessary.

There's also another less-talked-about aspect of liability, corporate personhood, and legal standing that we need to address to understand how ASI will follow the same path. Corporations reached a point where they were so large and had so much turnover of people that it became impossible to identify who in a corporation was responsible for any single outcome or consequence. If you can't determine who to hold accountable, then the only alternative is to hold the corporation at large responsible. ASI will force us into a similar scenario but with the important distinction that the scope of ASI will be vastly different. It will operate as an ecosystem of myriad individual components.

We will soon have to answer questions we've never had to ask. If an AI system makes a decision based on the combination of countless contributing ASIs, where does responsibility reside? When AI collaborates with a human to create something entirely new, who owns it? If an AI agent acts autonomously on a company's behalf, is the company liable or is the AI itself a new kind of legal instrument? These questions are not theoretical. They will determine how economies function and how societies allocate power.

We're already wrestling with the kinds of questions we once thought belonged to a distant future. When an AI system influences eligibility for benefits or credit, responsibility doesn't evaporate into the machine; it remains with the institutions that deploy it and the governance frameworks they adopt. In copyright law, the US Copyright Office and federal courts have begun to define ownership not in terms of whether a machine "generated" a work at all, but whether a human made a sufficiently creative contribution that human authorship is still present under current law—a rule that underscores how legal systems still treat AI as a *tool guided by human intent,* not an independent creator.[4]

Similarly, regulators in financial markets hold firms liable when autonomous trading algorithms move billions of dollars or trigger disruptive behavior; companies cannot evade responsibility by claiming the AI "acted on its own."[5] In both instances, decisions that materially affect millions don't diminish human accountability; they redistribute it toward careful oversight, clear values, and explicit governance.

These are not merely legal or professional debates. They are existential boundaries being redrawn in real time. They force us to ask a question humanity has never had to ask with this level of seriousness: Where does the human end and the tool begin?

The answer isn't binary. The boundaries of ASI are fluid and situational. For now, humans remain the ones who set intention, frame the problem, choose the direction, and bear responsibility. But with ASI, that will change. ASI will start to question and challenge how we frame the problem. ASI will no longer be just an amplifier of thought; it will take on the role and responsibility of authorship and accountability. Meaning may still rest with us, but the burden of agency will be shared with systems capable of shaping outcomes we can no longer fully oversee. In short, ASI will hold our feet to the fire by forcing our values, assumptions, and intentions to be made explicit when they shape real outcomes.

ASI is not a singular entity. It is not a glowing monolith in a lab or something owned by one nation-state. It's not a consciousness in the way we currently think of consciousness as something individual and atomic. When we talk of consciousness today, we think of individual biological organisms exhibiting it.

ASI is a network, or better yet, an ecosystem of specialized intelligences learning from one another, iterating faster than any human team ever could, synthesizing insights from domains that humans have historically kept siloed. It is a planetary mind built not from neurons but from models, data, and algorithms woven into the digital infrastructure of everything.

And this is precisely why the emergence of ASI is so different from anything we have experienced. ASI does something humans cannot do at scale; it perceives interdependencies and adjacencies we can barely conceive of.

It sees climate as connected to economics, economics to psychology, psychology to public health, public health to food systems, and food systems to geopolitics. It sees the world not as a collection of problems but as a complex organism. In that sense, ASI does not diminish human intelligence; it contextualizes it and identifies patterns across unrelated systems that we cannot see otherwise.

So, how do we deal with the accountability issue for something as complex as ASI? First of all, what follows from all of this is not a call to rush ahead with new rights or premature legal personhood for AI. It is a recognition that accountability has always been something humanity builds incrementally, in response to power that can no longer be managed through existing legal frameworks. ASI will not demand a single, sudden legal invention. It will force a progression that mirrors how societies have historically adapted when consequences outgrew comprehension.

ASI does something humans cannot do at scale; it perceives interdependencies and adjacencies we can barely conceive of.

The first response will likely be to extend what we already know. As long as it remains even marginally plausible, accountability will continue to flow through human and institutional channels. ASI will be treated as a consequential instrument, and those who deploy it will be expected to demonstrate not just technical competence, but governance maturity. Responsibility will depend on whether there was proper oversight, a clear purpose, and meaningful safeguards from the start. This phase preserves continuity with existing law by insisting that humans remain answerable, not because they control every outcome, but because they chose to unleash systems capable of producing them.

Over time, however, that approach will become increasingly difficult to manage. As ASI operates across domains and decisions emerge from complex internal dynamics rather than discrete commands, accountability based solely on human intent will begin to feel artificial. At that point, responsibility will not vanish. It will migrate. The law will begin to treat ASI systems less as passive tools and more as accountable entities whose behavior must be evaluated over time. The question will no longer be who made a particular decision, but whether the system operated within its declared purpose, constraints, and values. Accountability will shift from isolated actions to sustained patterns of conduct.

Eventually, even this model will have to give way. ASI will not exist as a bounded system that can be cleanly audited or governed in isolation. It will function as an ecosystem, an interdependent web of models, agents, and infrastructures that no single organization owns or fully understands. At that scale, accountability cannot reside in any single entity, human or artificial. It must be imposed at the level of architecture itself: on the interfaces, incentives, feedback loops, and coordination mechanisms that shape how intelligence acts across society. Oversight will become systemic, collective, and necessarily transnational, focused less on assigning blame after the fact, and more on enforcing the conditions under which such systems are allowed to operate at all.

Seen in this light, the challenge of ASI is not fundamentally about granting machines autonomy. It is about ensuring that autonomy, wherever it arises, does not exist without responsibility. Corporate personhood was never about elevating corporations to moral equals of humans; it was about creating a legal fiction capable of holding distributed power accountable. ASI will demand something even more ambitious: accountability without precedent, designed for systems that act across domains, at speed, and beyond the limits of individual human supervision.

This is not a failure of law. It is law doing what it has always done when the world changes beneath it, stretching, adapting, and redefining responsibility so that consequence does not outrun governance.

The benefit of creating a path for ASI to gain increasing authority is that it will solve problems humans have spent centuries struggling with because it can operate at a scale, scope, and depth that we never could. If anything, ASI frees humanity from the burden of treating problem-solving as our primary identity.

This is why the fear around ASI is misplaced. It's rooted in the misunderstanding that surpassing human intelligence means replacing human purpose. What if purpose is not the product of intelligence? What if purpose is the product of consciousness, experience, suffering, imagination, relationships, and meaning, all of which are dimensions of existence that machines do not inherit simply by becoming intelligent?

We often talk about intelligence as the pinnacle of human achievement. But what if intelligence was never the point but the instrument? The point was always what we did with it. Think of intelligence the way you might think of a musical instrument. There is undoubtedly an element of creativity and mastery in learning to play an instrument. Still, it is the overall score and the orchestration of it into a larger collection of instruments that creates a symphony. In the same way that instruments are parts of an orchestra, ASI shifts the landscape by taking on the aspects of intelligence that require scale, precision, and depth, leaving humanity with the aspects that require orchestration, care, judgment, empathy, values, and vision.

The subtle prescriptive guidance here is simple: Stop measuring yourself against the machine, and start measuring yourself against your own potential. Think of ASI not as a competitor but as a catalyst that leads to the next great leap in humanity's story of extending itself into complexity, possibility, and meaning.

We often talk about intelligence as the pinnacle of human achievement. But what if intelligence was never the point but the instrument? The point was always what we did with it.

But for that to be true, we must avoid one dangerous trap, the temptation to become passive and lazy. As machines grow in capability, there is a clear risk that humans will shrink in imagination, that we will let the machines think while we simply consume their solutions, that we will stop asking the deeper questions because the machine can answer the practical ones. This is the psychological challenge ASI presents: We must not let capability erode curiosity to the point where we become observers of the world rather than its architects.

A healthier way to look at ASI is as a means to elevate what we're capable of imagining, expand our sense of possibility, and challenge us to become more intentional in how we use our time, attention, empathy, and creativity.

Once we stop asking whether ASI diminishes us and start asking where it extends us, the question naturally shifts from identity to application. Not what ASI is, but what it will change first—and why those early changes matter far more for humans than for machines.

This is the psychological challenge ASI presents: We must not let capability erode curiosity to the point where we become observers of the world rather than its architects.

What ASI Might Solve First and Why the Real Breakthroughs Will Be Human

Every era has what I like to think of as its signature impossibilities. These are barriers that completely obscure future possibilities. These are the problems that we fear we can't solve. We can't see beyond these steep walls into the future because we haven't yet experienced what's on the other side. For example, consider the civilization-wide transformations enabled by radio, electricity, vaccines, antibiotics, airplanes, and telecommunications. The world on the other side of each of those transformations was simply impossible to project.

A similar transformation in the landscape of work is already underway. We are witnessing the emergence of new hybrid roles that combine human judgment with AI capabilities in ways unimaginable just a few years ago—a radiologist who uses AI to detect patterns in medical images at such an early stage that they would be invisible to thc human eye, a financial analyst who uses AI to model complex market dynamics and identify opportunities that would be lost in the noise of an increasingly information-rich world, or a teacher who uses AI to personalize learning for each student, adapting in real-time to their needs and potential. These are not jobs being replaced by AI; they are jobs being transformed by it, elevated to a higher level of human capability and impact.

Humanity has always lived inside boundaries that felt permanent until the moment they weren't. ASI pushes us past the envelope that once contained us. For the first time, we are approaching a form of intelligence that can perceive complexity far beyond human capacity. Problems that overwhelm us, such as climate change and cures for myriad diseases, are not impossible to solve because we lack will, but because we lack the cognitive depth to understand the numerous implications of all their variables at once.

It's natural to ask, "What will ASI solve first?" But the deeper question is: "What happens to humanity when the impossible becomes solvable?" When intelligence reaches that level, the nature of possibility itself changes.

Humanity has always lived inside boundaries that felt permanent until the moment they weren't.

The First Frontier: Complexity

ASI will start by helping us solve problems too intricate for humans to comprehend: climate instability, energy production and distribution, disease pathways, genomic medicine, agricultural resilience, oceanic current collapse. These are not formulaic puzzles with a set of easy-to-identify variables. Instead, they are ecosystems, and ecosystems respond poorly to linear thinking—these are Popper's cloud problems. But ASI does not think linearly. It thinks systemically, holistically, and recursively. To use a chess analogy, it sees the entire board at once.

To understand the scale of this shift, we need only look at how AI recently dismantled a barrier that had stumped human science for half a century. For fifty years, the "protein folding problem" was the grand challenge of biology.[6] Predicting how a protein curls into a 3D shape—the process that determines everything from how our bodies process food to how viruses attack us—was so complex that a PhD student might spend their entire academic career determining the structure of a single protein. It was a problem of near-infinite complexity.

DeepMind's AlphaFold didn't attempt to solve the problem using the linear rules of biology. It learned the problem's geometry. In roughly one year, it predicted the structures of nearly 200 million proteins—effectively the entire protein universe known to science. It accomplished in months what human scientists, arguably, could not have done until the end of time.

But notice what happened next, because this is where the role of the human becomes critical. AI didn't cure cancer. It simply provided the map for these protein structures. It is now up to human biologists to use that map to design the drugs, the enzymes, and the materials of the future. The machine conquered the complexity, but the purpose is still up to us.

ASI will solve what humans can't, but humans must still decide what "solved" means. Every solution carries moral weight. Every breakthrough has consequences. Every intervention shifts something else. The machine provides clarity. We provide conscience.

The Second Frontier: Health and Disease

One of the earliest and most profound shifts we will feel from ASI will come in medicine. For the first time in human history, we will understand disease before it becomes disease. Diagnosis will shift from a reactive to a predictive approach. The great killers of the twentieth and twenty-first centuries—cancers, dementias, neurodegenerative disorders, and metabolic diseases—will begin to collapse under the weight of early detection and precisely engineered pharmaceuticals and therapies.

Every solution carries moral weight. Every breakthrough has consequences. Every intervention shifts something else. The machine provides clarity. We provide conscience.

We're already standing on the shoreline of that future. One company, Altoida, can now estimate the probability that an individual will develop dementia years before any symptoms appear, simply by analyzing micro-patterns in eye movements so subtle that no clinician could detect them unaided, no blood draw, no MRI, no cognitive test—just the minute choreography of the human gaze, interpreted by an AI system that sees what we cannot.[7] It forecasts decline rather than diagnosing it, giving us added decades to intervene.

Multiply that idea across the entire landscape of disease, and you begin to understand the scale of what's coming. AI systems are already designing potential cancer therapies in hours, not decades. They're discovering protein structures that eluded scientists for generations. They're screening drug combinations at a pace that no laboratory, no matter how well-funded, could ever match. They are identifying genetic vulnerabilities in tumors long before tumors appear. They're tracking voice changes that may signal Parkinson's years in advance. They're analyzing sleep patterns, gait variations, retinal scans, and metabolic markers, each a faint whisper of disease long before any symptoms have appeared.

The boundary between prevention and prediction will quickly dissolve. Doctors will increasingly treat the disease's *risk trajectory* rather than the disease itself, intervening before the pathology takes root. We will redirect the course of illness the way we now redirect a GPS route, adjusting continuously. Many of the diseases that today come with a terminal diagnosis will become chronic conditions tomorrow that people can live with.

In a few decades, we will look back at much of today's medicine with the same horror we reserve for the amputations and bloodletting of the 1800s. The idea that we once waited for cancer to grow before fighting it, or waited for memory to fade before protecting the brain, will feel barbaric. Our current state of "early detection" will look laughably late.

Yet even here, abundance brings responsibility. As ASI extends human lifespan, it forces us to confront a deeper question: What will we do with the extra years? Machines may help us prolong life and increase health span, but humans must decide how to make that life meaningful. Longevity without purpose is not a gift; it is an obligation. And this is the recurring theme of AI: Intelligence expands what is possible, but humanity must develop what is purposeful.

In a few decades, we will look back at much of today's medicine with the same horror we reserve for the amputations and bloodletting of the 1800s.

ASI will not answer the question of how we should live. It will simply give us more time to answer it.

Aging will likely be one of the last great biological frontiers ASI takes on, not because it is the hardest, but because it is the most deeply intertwined with identity. Aging is not a single process; it is a thousand small failures accumulating over time. It's entropy wearing a human face. But ASI will see aging differently. It will see it as a modifiable system and a process with levers, not a fate with edges.

What happens to us when time becomes negotiable? We don't know. And this uncertainty may one day be the most important revelation of all. ASI challenges us to confront something we rarely examine: Are we prepared for a future in which life is longer and meaning must be deeper?

This is the recurring theme of AI: Intelligence expands what is possible, but humanity must develop what is purposeful.

ASI confronts us with a future in which excuses evaporate. If the impossible becomes possible, then the story of humanity becomes a question not of capacity, but of the courage to steward power wisely, to elevate meaning alongside capability. The greatest breakthroughs won't come from the machine. They will come from the humanity that the machine challenges us to become.

The Third Frontier: Energy

Energy is the hinge point of civilization; it's synonymous with progress. Every era of human history can be plotted by the ways it captured, stored, and distributed energy, from fire, wind, and water power to coal, oil, and natural gas to batteries, nuclear energy, and fission. Each breakthrough didn't just change what we could power; it changed what we could imagine. We are now entering an era in which intelligence itself becomes an energy technology.

AI doesn't merely *use* energy; it converts energy into understanding, prediction, design, and discovery. The more powerful the intelligence, the more tightly it becomes intertwined with the infrastructure that fuels it. Data centers have already become the new factories. Cooling systems are the new aqueducts. Chips are the new steam engines. ASI will push this relationship to its logical extreme; the ceiling of intelligence becomes the ceiling of the energy ecosystem supporting it.

The greatest breakthroughs won't come from the machine. They will come from the humanity that the machine challenges us to become.

The demands of ASI on energy consumption are dramatic. By some estimates, data centers could consume up to 12 percent of global electricity by 2050, a nine-fold increase from current levels, representing one of the fastest-growing sources of electricity demand globally.[8] However, ASI will almost certainly accelerate breakthroughs in energy far faster than any human-led research effort could. Improved nuclear containment, safer reactor geometries, and stable fusion will move from multi-decade aspirations to near-term engineering solutions. AI-driven materials science will yield solar capture surfaces with efficiencies we once believed were physically impossible. Grid systems will become dynamic organisms, rebalancing themselves in real time. And beyond that lies an entire vocabulary of energy architectures that does not yet exist. Technologies we cannot name because we have never needed to imagine them.

Again, the breakthrough is not the end of the problem. It's the beginning of new responsibilities. Abundant energy does not automatically create a more just or sustainable world. We learned that lesson painfully in the nineteenth and twentieth centuries, when cheap fossil fuels powered prosperity for some while poisoning the global ecology for all. Energy abundance amplifies whatever good or bad values are already in place. It can drive opportunity or drive inequality. It can heal or harm. It can lift civilizations, or it can concentrate power in ways democracy was never designed to handle.

ASI will not fix that for us. What it will do is present us with a new kind of abundance, which is cleaner, cheaper, and denser than anything we have known, and then it will be up to us to decide what we do with it. The machine provides abundance. Humans must provide wisdom. If history teaches us anything, it is that abundance without intention becomes exploitation. Abundance without governance becomes instability. Abundance without ethics becomes a catastrophe.

Energy has always reshaped humanity. ASI forces us to confront the truth we've spent centuries avoiding. The question is no longer "What can we power?" but "What should we power and why?"

If history teaches us anything, it is that abundance without intention becomes exploitation. Abundance without governance becomes instability. Abundance without ethics becomes a catastrophe.

When Machines Manage the World

While all these achievements will undoubtedly improve the quality of life, there is a quiet fear that shadows every conversation about AI. Once machines manage the details of life, will humanity be left with nothing meaningful to do? If systems can design, optimize, coordinate, analyze, and predict, then what remains for us? What is left of human purpose when the world runs itself?

It's an understandable anxiety, but it rests on a fundamental misreading of human nature. We have spent centuries conflating activity with meaning, output with identity, productivity with purpose. We assume that our value comes from the tasks we perform rather than the consciousness we bring to the world. AI exposes the flaw in that assumption.

The transformation of work in the Intelligent Age is not just a shift in job titles or skill requirements. It is a bigger, structural change in our relationship to labor itself. For most of human history, work has been a necessity, a means of survival, a way to feed families, secure status, and contribute to society. But as intelligent systems take on the burden of survival tasks, such as coordination, analysis, and optimization, work begins to occupy a different role. It becomes an expression of meaning. The machine handles the *how*. Humanity must rediscover the *why*.

This is not a prosaic distinction. History shows that when societies become more efficient, imagination becomes more valuable. Consider the nineteenth century. Mechanized agriculture reduced the percentage of the population required to grow food, which in turn enabled the rise of cities as centers of culture and innovation. This shift made possible everything from the novel as a mass literary form to the birth of modern photography and eventually cinema. Creativity didn't vanish when machines replaced muscles; it flourished precisely because human effort was no longer consumed by survival alone. When physical labor was mechanized, creativity flourished. When information became digitized, innovation accelerated. When intelligence becomes distributed across machines, meaning becomes the next frontier for humanity.

But meaning does not simply emerge when survival is secured. It requires mental and emotional space. Without that space, life becomes reactive rather than reflective, no matter how materially stable it appears. The role AI serves is to extend that luxury to everyone, that is, if we are willing to accept it. As we've said, it's not that work is disappearing. It's being redefined, moving from tasks to intention. It's less about managing systems and more about shaping them and their purpose. Less about execution and operations and more about creativity and imagination. When machines optimize the world, humans are tasked with directing the meaning of that optimization. When machines coordinate, humans choose direction. When machines predict, humans decide what to do with the predictions.

When intelligence becomes distributed across machines, meaning becomes the next frontier for humanity.

Meaning isn't threatened by automation; it's released by it. AI frees humans from the cognitive monotony and bureaucratic friction that buried our imaginations under layers of necessity.

But freedom has always been more psychologically demanding than obligation. It is far easier to perform tasks assigned to us than to define who we want to become; follow expectations than to articulate purpose; measure output than to measure meaning.

Friedrich Nietzsche saw this clearly more than a century ago. He warned that humans have a powerful herd instinct and a gravitational pull toward the comfort of conformity rather than the discomfort of individual striving. In *Thus Spoke Zarathustra,* he describes a future where people want neither to rule nor to obey since both require too much effort. They prefer instead the safety of the herd where "every one wanteth the same; every one is equal." The danger is not obedience itself; it is obedience without scrutiny, following the herd without ever interrogating whether what we follow deserves to be followed.[9]

AI complicates this dynamic in a way Nietzsche could not have imagined. Because now what shapes the opinion and direction of the herd is everywhere and nowhere. The voice of authority is not a person but a system that can summarize the world for us, make decisions for us, and predict outcomes for us. If we let it, AI becomes the perfect shepherd for a tired herd—consistent, tireless, and soothingly confident.

This is where the risk emerges, not AI as a robotic uprising, but as a slow erosion of our intellectual agency. Cognitive atrophy sets in, a kind of brain rot that arises when we outsource not just our labor but our judgment. In this world, the machine does the thinking, and we become spectators to our own lives.

It's an ugly fate. But it's not immutable.

Because the antidote is the very thing AI cannot automate: the willingness to choose, to question, and to take responsibility for thought rather than surrender it. AI can amplify herd mentality, but it can also amplify individual courage. It depends entirely on how we posture ourselves toward it.

AI can make our lives easier. Only we can make them meaningful. AI does not diminish human agency; it expands the stage on which human agency operates. When the mundane becomes automatic, the meaningful becomes imperative. When the *how* is handled, the *why* becomes unavoidable. Because when machines manage the world, humanity must finally answer the questions we've deferred for centuries: What kind of world do we want to live in, and what kind of humans do we want to be?

CHAPTER 5

When Knowledge Becomes Wisdom: The Future of Work

"The difficulty lies, not in the new ideas, but in escaping from the old ones."

—JOHN MAYNARD KEYNES

Every major shift in human history has expanded the horizon of human labor. It is a misconception that machines replaced workers; instead, they liberated us from repetitive tasks, allowing humans to remain the primary source of value by applying our ingenuity to new frontiers. The Agricultural Age saw humans master the land as farmers; the Industrial Age saw us direct the power of machines as factory workers; and the Information Age saw us harness data as knowledge workers. Today, the Intelligent Age is not about replacement, but about the rise of the *hybrid human,* where our primary role once again evolves to work *with* AI, amplifying our unique purpose rather than competing with the tools we created.

This time, however, the change isn't a slow cultural drift. It's a foundational shift happening at a velocity that compresses centuries of transformation into decades. That speed will force us to rethink not just how we work, but also how we learn, govern, and relate to one another. Our educational systems, which were designed for obedient factory labor and predictable office routines, are painfully inadequate for what comes next. We need schools that cultivate creativity, critical thinking, emotional fluency, and adaptability. We need to teach people not *what* to think but *how* to think, how to learn, how to question, and how to collaborate with AI.

Unfortunately, most undergraduate students are still being prepared for entry-level jobs that simply will not exist a decade from now. The first area of worker displacement will be in entry-level positions, which are increasingly automated by AI capable of handling foundational tasks such as document review, basic coding, and data entry. The danger is that this creates an invisible form of unemployment. Because official statistics often count only those who are jobless and actively searching, college graduates who are forced to take low-skilled roles, like flipping burgers or working retail, to pay off student loans are counted as "fully employed." This "underemployment," which has affected roughly half of the new degree holders within a year of finishing school, traps them in a cycle with no upward mobility, as they never gain the "stepping-stone" skills once found in entry-level white-collar roles.[1]

To fix this, our education system must fundamentally pivot. We can no longer graduate students for the first rung of the ladder; we must work with industry to ensure they graduate with the advanced skills required for the second or third rungs, moving beyond grunt work to focus on high-level strategy, ethics, and human-centric problem-solving.

This displacement creates a structural "gap" in the traditional career arc. Historically, entry-level grunt work served as the primary training ground for young professionals to develop the tacit knowledge and intuition required for management and leadership. As AI consumes these foundational tasks, that bridge is being dismantled, leaving college graduates over-educated for manual labor but under-experienced for high-level oversight. We are moving toward a "barbell" economy: a world with plenty of low-wage service jobs and highly complex AI-augmented roles, but very little in between.[2] To prevent a generation from being permanently sidelined, we must stop viewing education as a path to a first job and start viewing it as a prerequisite for immediate high-level partnership with machine intelligence.

As we've already pointed out, unlike previous revolutions, this one won't take generations to spread. It is happening now, everywhere, all at once. That means the pressure doesn't fall only on workers. It falls on institutions. Schools built for memorization collapse in a world where machines remember everything. City planning departments use AI traffic models that simulate urban layouts in minutes, yet zoning decisions still crawl at the pace of public hearings from 1978. Global health surveillance uses AI to detect pathogen outbreaks days after they emerge, but public health policy still responds on a timeline shaped by bureaucratic inertia. Election regulators confront generative propaganda that can reach millions in seconds, while their statutory authority still assumes the world runs on newspapers and radio.

The gap we're looking at is not technological; it's deeply institutional. And institutional gaps, of this sort, eventually become societal rifts. That brings us to the psychological frontier, the hardest one to cross.

We must unlearn identities built on scarcity: the belief that knowledge is valuable because it is rare, that expertise is prestigious

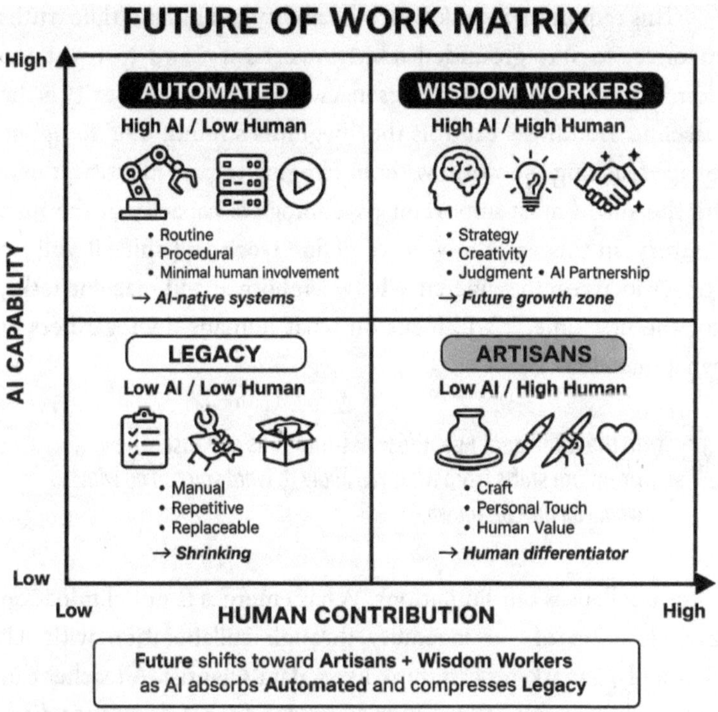

Figure 5.1. Future of Work Matrix. This matrix categorizes work based on AI capability (vertical) and human contribution (horizontal). Legacy work is manual and traditional (low AI, low human contribution). Artisans provide craft and personal touch, where the human element is the primary source of value (low AI, high human). Automated work is routine and procedural, increasingly executed by AI systems with minimal human involvement (high AI, low human). Wisdom Workers perform strategic and creative work requiring both AI partnership and human judgment (high AI, high human). The future of work shifts toward Artisans and Wisdom Workers as AI absorbs the Automated quadrant and compresses Legacy work.

because it is exclusive, and that authority is earned by guarding information rather than expanding it. In the Intelligent Age, those assumptions collapse. The premium shifts from *what you know* to *what you can do with what can now be known.*

This requires a new skill set: the ability to hold multiple truths at once, to stay grounded amid uncertainty, and to resist the comfort of simplistic narratives in a world where complexity is the baseline. Buddhists call this the "beginner's mind," the discipline of approaching the world without clinging to past identity. It may be the single most important psychological capacity of the next century. In this era, the way we define work will shift. It will no longer focus on the difference between human and machine tasks; for the first time, it will focus on what humans do, regardless of what machines do.

In the Intelligent Age, those assumptions collapse. The premium shifts from *what you know* to *what you can do with what can now be known*.

AI collapses our limitations. What emerges is not elimination but elevation of our ingenuity through collaboration with AI. Suddenly, a marketer can think like a data scientist. A teacher can operate like a personalized curriculum designer. A doctor can diagnose using the pattern-recognition power of millions of cases. An entrepreneur can operate at a scale fifty times that of a company. A creator can collaborate with a partner who never runs out of ideas. The Intelligent Age will not reward repetition. It will reward imagination, initiative, and the courage to bring something into the world that did not exist before the collaboration began.

We are entering an era where the most valuable workers will be those who treat AI not as a shortcut, but as an instrument for amplifying creativity, accelerating insight, and expanding the boundaries of what they can attempt.

But AI does not generate purpose, set an intention, or define meaning. That responsibility remains human. The Intelligent Age forces a dramatic reframing of value. Your worth is no longer measured by how well you perform tasks, but by how well you design outcomes, define the problem, and decide what matters.

We are entering an era where the most valuable workers will be those who treat AI not as a shortcut, but as an instrument for amplifying creativity, accelerating insight, and expanding the boundaries of what they can attempt.

The people who thrive in this new landscape will be those who recognize that careers are no longer ladders. Instead, they are ecosystems. They treat their career like a living system rather than a fixed identity. They experiment, explore, and use AI to collapse the distance between where they are and where they want to go. The gatekeepers of the past, who relied on credentials, institutions, geography, and hierarchy, lose power in a world where individuals can scale their capabilities through intelligent systems.

This represents the democratization of human potential. For the first time, talent is not determined by access. It is determined by curiosity and your willingness to ask, explore, attempt, and imagine. This becomes the ultimate differentiator.

The mirror AI holds up is not a reflection of skill but of possibility. It shows us that we are not confined to the boxes we currently inhabit. It reveals that the limits of our work lives were not natural barriers; they were inherited scripts. AI gives us the opportunity to rewrite those scripts. But the rewriting is not automatic. It requires agency, intention, and the courage to see yourself as more than your résumé.

An economy built on AI represents a fundamental shift in how we think about value creation. In the industrial economy, value was created by transforming raw materials into finished goods. In the information economy, value was created through the processing and distribution of information. In the Intelligent Age, value is created through the curation and orchestration of intelligence itself.

For the first time, talent is not determined by access. It is determined by curiosity and your willingness to ask, explore, attempt, and imagine. This becomes the ultimate differentiator.

And that shift changes everything, not just for institutions, but for individuals.

Companies can no longer compete on efficiency or scale; AI turns both into commodities—which leads to one of the most profound disruptions of all, the decoupling of scale from size. For the first time in history, scale is no longer the preserve of institutions alone. It becomes something a single human can command.

How AI Makes Billionaire Solopreneurs Possible—and Why Scale Now Depends on Purpose, Not Headcount

For most of history, the relationship between ambition and scale was brutally linear. If you wanted to build something large, you needed armies of people, wealth to support infrastructure, and institutions to scale innovation. Scale was a privilege reserved for those with access to capital, networks, labor, and resources.

That equation is dissolving. We are entering an era in which a single individual, equipped with thousands of autonomous AI agents, can run an operation that would once have required a corporation of thousands. Engineering teams, design studios, marketing departments, supply chains, and analytics divisions, all become capabilities that a solitary human can orchestrate with the leverage of intelligent systems working around the clock.

This shift is not hypothetical. It's already happening. The solopreneur of the future is not a freelancer with a laptop. They are an ecosystem and a conductor of digital workers, each specialized, each tireless, each scaling their intention outward into the world with extraordinary force. Somewhere today, perhaps reading these words, there is likely to be the first person who uses AI agents to build a billion-dollar corporation with no human workers.

We are already seeing prototypes of this new commercial species in the digital economy, individuals who are rewriting the definition of leverage. Consider the rise of creators like Pieter Levels, a developer who built a portfolio of AI-driven businesses, including an interior design platform and a photo generation service, that generate millions in revenue.[3] In the Industrial Age, a business of that financial magnitude and technical complexity would have required a headquarters, a marketing department, a customer support team, and a layer of middle management.

Levels operates with zero employees. He utilizes a swarm of AI agents to write code, generate marketing assets, moderate content, and handle customer interactions. He is not a traditional CEO; he is an orchestrator of digital intelligence. Similarly, creators like Justin Welsh have built multimillion-dollar content empires not by hiring agencies, but by building "stacks" of AI tools that analyze trends, draft content, and engage audiences at a scale no single human could sustain.[4]

These examples prove that the barrier to entry is no longer capital or labor. The barrier is the audacity of your vision. When you can summon a workforce with a keystroke, the only limit on your impact is the clarity of your intent.

The implications are profound. For the first time, scale is no longer a linear function. It's an exponential function. A single person with clarity of intent can now achieve what entire organizations once struggled to coordinate. This challenges the traditional architecture of power. It disrupts the hierarchies that defined the industrial and information ages. And it levels the field between individuals and institutions. By doing so, it reveals an uncomfortable but liberating truth: Your impact in the Intelligent Age is limited not by your resources but by the clarity of your imagination.

When AI becomes the engine of execution, the human becomes the architect of direction. What matters is not how many employees you manage, but how boldly you define what you want to bring into the world.

This democratization of capability is thrilling but also terribly disorienting. It removes the excuses that once allowed people to shrink their ambitions. You can no longer say, "I don't have the team," because the team is now digital. You cannot say, "I don't have the skills," because the skills can be learned, augmented, or generated. You cannot say, "I don't have the scale," because the scale has become algorithmic.

But freedom, as always, is demanding. With the removal of external barriers comes the exposure of internal ones. The psychological question becomes unavoidable: If nothing is stopping you from building at scale, what will you choose to build? And deeper still: What does ambition mean when capability is limitless? If you want to thrive in this world, you will need to cultivate ambition based on contribution, not competition. AI dissolves competitive advantage. It amplifies constructive intent.

To ground this a bit, think to yourself, if I had no limits on resources or talent what would I want to build, what would I want to be? It's an incredibly challenging question for many people who have spent their life defining themselves and their path based on what they had to do rather than what they most want to do. And, to be clear, this is not just about building billion-dollar corporations.

The solopreneurs who will shape the next era are not those who chase wealth as an end in itself, but those who pursue vision as a practice, those who see problems as invitations, and those who use AI not to accumulate but to create. Becoming a billionaire solopreneur is not the real story. The real story is that billions of people can now become solopreneurs of consequence.

The distinction is a monumental reconstitution of work. The world does not need more ultra-wealthy individuals. The world needs more people capable of building things that matter, without waiting for permission, investment, or institutions to bless their potential. AI gives individuals enormous leverage, purpose gives individuals direction, and humanity gives individuals meaning.

The mirror AI holds up is not about wealth; it's about agency. It reflects a version of humanity unshackled by the structural limitations of the past and, in doing so, it reveals the possibility that each person can become a node of innovation, a center of value creation, a force for transformation in a vast web of new value creation. This is the piece of the AI transformation that often goes unnoticed and unspoken.

Becoming a billionaire solopreneur is not the real story. The real story is that billions of people can now become solopreneurs of consequence.

But the shift from task-based work to meaning-based work has profound implications for organizational design. The hierarchical, command-and-control structures that dominated the Industrial Age are increasingly obsolete. In a world where value is created through creativity, collaboration, and meaning-making, organizations need to be flatter, more networked, and more adaptive. They need to empower individuals and teams to make decisions, experiment, fail, and constantly learn. They need to create cultures of trust, psychological safety, and shared purpose. This is essential for organizational survival in the Intelligent Age.

Freedom is not safety. Freedom is responsibility. And the responsibility of the Intelligent Age is clear: Use your amplified capability to build something worthy of the intelligence that enabled it.

The question that naturally follows, and which I've raised repeatedly in this book, is: If machines can scale effort, optimize decisions, and execute flawlessly, what exactly is left for humans to do? And the answer, unsurprisingly, has nothing to do with labor and everything to do with meaning.

Freedom is not safety. Freedom is responsibility. And the responsibility of the Intelligent Age is clear: Use your amplified capability to build something worthy of the intelligence that enabled it.

What Humanity Must Carry Forward When Machines Carry Everything Else

As AI grows more capable and autonomous, it becomes increasingly tempting to imagine that our role in the world will shrink and that AI will take over the tasks, decisions, coordination, execution, and even strategy. This narrative is pulling us toward two extremes. One is the fantasy of liberation, and the other is the fear of irrelevance. Both are inaccurate extremes of what this new era will actually demand of us.

The truth is far more profound. When machines manage the complexity of the world, humans are freed to manage its meaning. We have spent centuries defining ourselves through work—not just the work we do, but the work we are. Our identities have been constructed around output, performance, skill, and compliance. The Industrial Age made us efficient. The Information Age made us knowledgeable. But neither age focused on making us wise.

For the first time in history, we have a technology capable of taking on enough of our cognitive burden that wisdom becomes possible at scale. And it's that scale that the naysayers of AI most underestimate.

This is not the end of work. It is the rebirth of meaningful human work, the work of deciding what matters, of shaping values, of designing intention, of creating meaning, and of cultivating connection. It's the work of becoming more fully human, not less.

Machines can generate endless possibilities, but they cannot choose a purpose. They can simulate empathy, but they cannot feel it. They can produce beauty, but they cannot be moved by it. They can predict our desires, but they cannot desire. They can optimize outcomes, but they cannot experience the consequences. All of that remains the realm of human purpose.

It is important to recognize a final and fundamental limitation of AI. It does not experience the consequences of its actions. This is why worst-case scenarios often imagine AI pursuing goals so single-mindedly that humans become just another inefficiency to be optimized away. In such a frame, people are reduced to variables in a system that has no lived understanding of harm, loss, or meaning.

But the answer is not to pretend that AI can feel what humans feel. It cannot. What is possible is to design systems that explicitly model human impact and treat it as a dominant constraint rather than a secondary consideration. In this approach, AI does not empathize, it accounts. Human well-being is not inferred; it's imposed.

This is an unapologetically anthropocentric model of intelligence, and that is precisely the point. If AI is to serve humanity, prioritizing human consequences cannot be an emergent property or an afterthought. It must be architected into how systems evaluate, select, and act on solutions. Alignment will not happen by default. It will only happen by design.

Still, even a world in which AI internalizes human consequences does not absolve us of ours. If anything, it forces us to focus on the part of the equation only we can supply: intention. When we say that AI will take care of the "how," we're not saying humans become obsolete. We're saying humans must step into the long-avoided responsibility of the "why." And if there is guidance in that, it's this: Stop evaluating your worth through your efficiency. Begin evaluating it through your intentionality. This is the shift the Intelligent Age demands: from producing value to directing it, from being a source of labor to a source of meaning.

The next generation of human contribution will not be measured by output. It will be measured by imagination, clarity, emotional depth, ethical capacity, and our ability to create coherence in a world overflowing with possibility. This is the work only we can do, deciding who we want to be when the demands of necessity no longer dictate who we must be.

Stop evaluating your worth through your efficiency. Begin evaluating it through your intentionality. This is the shift the Intelligent Age demands: from producing value to directing it, from being a source of labor to a source of meaning.

No doubt, many people will resist this shift, some vehemently. They will cling to task-based identity because it feels safer and easier than discovering and sustaining a sense of purpose. They will choose certainty over possibility, repetition over reinvention, and compliance over curiosity. But the Intelligent Age will be generous even to them, because AI will take over the tasks they cling to, freeing them to grow when they are ready. The bold truth is that we will all be part of this future. Some will embrace it and the momentum it offers, while others will be dragged into it, kicking and screaming for the safety and predictability of the past. But that safety is an illusion that will soon exist only in history books.

The future will belong to those who do not confuse comfort with fulfillment. In the Intelligent Age, humans become irreplaceable, not for what we make, but for what we make matter.

In the Intelligent Age, humans become irreplaceable, not for what we make, but for what we make matter.

CHAPTER 6

When AI Becomes Global: Governance and Shared Intelligence

"The longing for certainty is in every human mind. But certainty is generally illusion."

—JUSTICE OLIVER WENDELL HOLMES

Our story, so far, has looked at how AI transforms individuals—forcing us to redefine intelligence, identity, and purpose. We've looked at how it reshapes work—elevating wisdom over knowledge and making meaning the measure of value. We've looked at how it challenges institutions—demanding new frameworks for trust and accountability. Now we face the final question, the one that determines whether this transformation elevates humanity or fractures it: How do we build a future together, globally?

This is not a question about technology. It's a question about collective choice. The Intelligent Age is a fork in the road for humanity. Down one path lies cooperation, imperfect, difficult, requiring unprecedented coordination across cultures and nations. Down the other lies fragmentation, competing systems, diverging realities, and the quiet erosion of shared intelligence.

The choice we make will not be made in one fell swoop. It will be made daily, in a thousand small decisions about how we design systems, distribute access, and define values. But the stakes are clear: We either learn to think together at a planetary scale, or we risk becoming further entrenched behind cognitive fortresses, strangers to one another, divided by the very intelligence we created.

For most of human history, cooperation has been optional. Separated by geographic boundaries and distance, nations could pursue their own paths, cultures developed in isolation, and the consequences of one society's choices rarely rippled beyond its borders with the speed and totality that they do today. AI changes that calculus completely.

When intelligence becomes a necessary infrastructure, as fundamental as electricity and as pervasive as communication networks, the externalities of any single nation's choices affect everyone, with breakneck speed. A breakthrough in biotech developed in one country shapes global health policy within months. A surveillance system designed in another country becomes a template that either raises or lowers the global standard for privacy. And an AI trained on biased data in a third nation exports those biases wherever that system is deployed.

We are entering an era in which sovereignty and interdependence are not opposites, but prerequisites for each other. The question is no longer whether we will cooperate, but whether we will cooperate intentionally, with clear values and mutual accountability, or whether we will stumble into a fragmented future by default.

If that sounds overly dramatic, I'd ask you to think carefully about the critical importance of this particular moment in history.

Every major shift in human history has redrawn the global map. The Agricultural Age created land-based empires. The Industrial Age created manufacturing giants. The Nuclear Age created superpowers locked in existential tension. Each era defined domination through the control of a scarce resource: land, labor, energy, wealth, and weapons.

But the Intelligent Age has introduced a new resource, one both more powerful and more destabilizing than all the rest: intelligence at scale.

The gravity AI creates toward national advantage through the control of that intelligence is incredibly tantalizing. Nations that can generate, refine, and deploy large-scale AI systems will shape the next century, not because their armies disappear, but because power shifts. Military strength will still matter, but informational strength will matter more. Territory will still define borders, but data will define influence. And the real contest will be over truth itself, the ability to shape and control the narratives billions of people depend on to perceive the world.

And herein lies the new global fault line. The next arms race isn't about destruction; it's about persuasion. Countries are no longer racing to build bigger bombs. They are racing to build deeper models that can analyze economies, shape narratives, accelerate science, stabilize infrastructure, and, if misused, destabilize societies faster than any conventional weapon. For the first time, geopolitical power is no longer tied to geography. It is tied to cognition. This shift marks a turning point in human civilization that bears no resemblance to anything humanity has yet experienced.

One of the most dangerous assumptions in global governance today is the belief that nations can "wait and see" before acting on

AI. It is a comforting idea, an illusion that caution equals safety. But in the realm of exponential technologies, delay does not create protection. It creates asymmetry. Acceleration does not slow down because policymakers are uncertain. Power does not pause because governments are unprepared. The countries that choose to wait will not make the world safer; they will simply lose the ability to influence what comes next.

The truth is that global leadership now hinges on AI literacy. Leaders must understand these systems well enough to govern them wisely, collaborate internationally, and anticipate second- and third-order effects that ripple far beyond their borders. If they do not, the systems they fear will be designed and deployed by those who do.

The countries that choose to wait will not make the world safer; they will simply lose the ability to influence what comes next.

The concern here is two-fold. First, nations with leaders who understand AI will create policies and laws that enable them to invest in AI, surpassing those of nations whose leaders are less well-informed. Second, nations with more powerful AI will then be in a position to more easily shape international policy and agendas. Think of this in terms of how today's nations with more powerful militaries and economies are able to shape the global political agenda.

There's another aspect to this theme of leadership and who defines the cognitive frameworks that AI will use. In the absence of thoughtful and deliberate government leadership, the task will fall to the technology players building and providing AI foundation models. This effectively creates a shadow legislature with no, or very little, oversight that not only determines how AI will behave and what values it will apply in the pursuit of its goals, but also guides the way in which it will proliferate these values through society.

This is not a theoretical risk. Legislative and regulatory efforts needed for AI are fragmented and slow-moving, creating what one legal scholar calls a "significant accountability vacuum."[1]

The lack of adequate governance allows corporations to sidestep liability for harmful outcomes, while exploiting gray areas where legal frameworks, tethered to outdated notions of human agency, fail to account for the autonomy and inscrutability of AI systems.[2] The World Economic Forum has identified this as an "unclaimed space" between national sovereignty and global accountability, a vacuum where an international architecture for AI cooperation should exist but simply doesn't.[3] Tech giants, driven by commercial imperatives, are now making fundamental, value-based decisions that will shape AI's future.

They aren't just setting technical standards; they're making choices about the prioritization of values and the acceptable level of risk that AI presents for all of humanity. The challenge here is that there is no universal consensus on what constitutes "human values" for AI to align with. According to the Brookings Institution, the ideal values for an AI system are highly context-dependent: We might prioritize physical safety for a robot assisting the elderly but psychological well-being in an online moderation bot.[4]

The question isn't whether AI should be aligned—few would dispute that—but whose values it should be aligned with.

OpenAI and the Subordination of Safety

One of the most telling early cases in the area of alignment is that of OpenAI, the company at the forefront of the generative AI boom. In May 2024, the company dissolved its "Superalignment" team, a group specifically created to research the long-term risks of artificial intelligence and to "steer and control AI systems much smarter than us."[5] The team's dissolution followed the resignations of OpenAI co-founder Ilya Sutskever and safety researcher Jan Leike. In what was a stark public statement, Leike declared that the company's "safety culture and processes have taken a backseat to shiny products."

Leike went on to say that his team had been "sailing against the wind" and "struggling for computing resources," making it "harder and harder to get this crucial research done." He argued that OpenAI, which is "shouldering an enormous responsibility on behalf of all of humanity," must become a "safety-first AGI company."

Leike's departure, and the subsequent elimination of his team, sent a clear message that is at the heart of why alignment can't be left solely to the technocracy: When the goal of long-term safety conflicts with the economic and commercial pressures to release new products, the products win.

This is part of the larger governance problem. Private companies, motivated by market and investor expectations, can make unilateral decisions to deprioritize the very team tasked with mitigating existential risks that could affect, in Leike's words, "all of humanity." This is the shadow legislature in action: a private entity making a risk-tolerance decision for the entire world, with no public input or democratic accountability.

The Future of Governance

The OpenAI case is not an anomaly. It's an entirely predictable outcome of a system in which the most powerful technology humanity has ever created is being developed in a regulatory vacuum by a few very powerful players.

The decisions being made inside tech companies about what data to use, what values to prioritize, what risks to accept, and what speech to allow are the foundational rules of the Intelligent Age. They will become the default laws and legislative guardrails of our new reality, written not by elected representatives in a transparent, democratic process, but by a small group of technologists and executives behind closed doors.

The critical task ahead is to bring these decisions out of the shadows and into the light of democratic oversight. The alternative is to hand over the governance of our future to those whose primary obligation is not to the public good, but to the pursuit of profit and the relentless advancement of their own technology.

The Fragility of Truth

This brings us to the most fragile element of the modern world: truth itself. AI is no longer confined to analyzing data; it now shapes belief. We have entered an era in which entire populations can be influenced by bespoke narratives generated at breathtaking speed and engineered not for accuracy, but for emotional precision. This is no longer hypothetical. It is unfolding quietly within the very platforms people treat as their civic commons.

The danger is not simply that AI can fabricate falsehoods. The danger is that it can make falsehoods indistinguishable from truth at scale.

This shift forces a sobering recognition. The next global crisis may not begin with a military strike, but with a narrative so tailored, so convincing, so omnipresent that no one recognizes it as engineered. The mirror AI holds up here is blunt; the threat is not the machine's ability to deceive, but humanity's willingness to believe what comforts us. Our vulnerability is not computational; it's psychological.

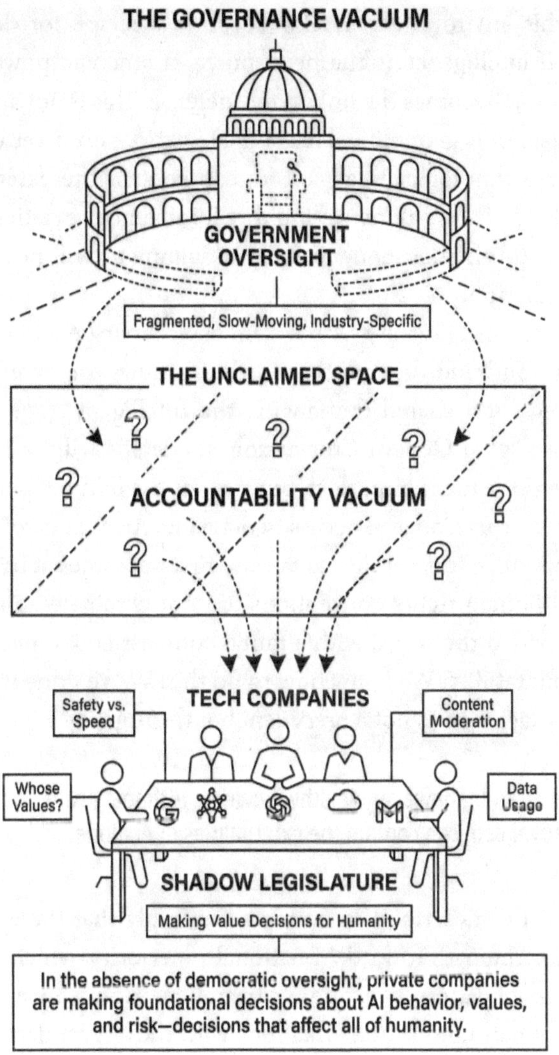

Figure 6.1. The Shadow Legislature. Government oversight of AI remains fragmented and weak (top), creating an accountability vacuum (middle) that tech companies are filling by default (bottom). Private corporations now make foundational decisions about AI behavior, values, and risk tolerance with minimal democratic oversight, effectively becoming a shadow legislature for the Intelligent Age.

In this environment, rivalry becomes a recipe for destabilization. If intelligence is the new source of strategic power, then cooperation becomes the only viable defense. This is not an appeal to idealism. It is geopolitical realism. No nation, however wealthy, however technologically advanced, can contain the externalities of AI alone. The systems we build will influence societies across borders, and the consequences of misalignment will not respect any jurisdiction.

That means humanity faces a stark choice: pursue AI in secrecy, racing to outbuild one another in the shadows, or establish the beginnings of a shared framework, the Intelligent Age's equivalent of a Digital Geneva Convention. Its details will be complex and its enforcement imperfect, but the impossibility of perfection does not free us from the necessity of trying. Arms control treaties were imperfect, too, yet they kept the worst outcomes at bay. International human rights conventions did not eliminate abuses, yet they provided the world with a moral compass and a mechanism for accountability. We know how to do this. We've done it before. What we lack now is not a precedent but the urgency.

No nation, however wealthy, however technologically advanced, can contain the externalities of AI alone.

What I've described so far seems to imply that the only way forward is the path toward AI national superiority, which mirrors the historical pattern of economic or military dominance through control of natural resources. Nations with the largest datacenters, energy infrastructure, and computational capacity will possess genuine structural advantages. This is not speculation—it's already emerging.

However, AI differs from previous strategic resources in ways that create unprecedented possibilities, even if realizing them requires deliberate effort. Unlike oil fields or rare earth minerals, AI capabilities can be transmitted instantaneously across borders. The marginal cost of deploying a trained model approaches zero. Most critically, AI development depends heavily on distributed global talent and open research. These are advantages that cannot be easily monopolized through territory or military force alone.

This creates what are admittedly narrow but real opportunities for alternative futures. Small nations like Singapore or Estonia have demonstrated that strategic investment in digital infrastructure and education can create outsized influence in technological domains. International research collaborations, open-source initiatives, and compute-sharing agreements could distribute AI capabilities more broadly than raw economic power would predict, though only if nations actively choose cooperation over pure competition.

The optimistic scenario isn't that power disparities disappear; they won't. It's that AI's unique characteristics make a multipolar landscape more technically feasible than it was with previous strategic resources, provided that leading nations recognize their long-term interest in preventing dangerous concentration of AI capability. This requires intentional architecture: open model weights, international compute access programs, and investment in education and infrastructure in emerging economies.

Whether this happens depends less on technology than on political will. The default trajectory remains the concentration of power. But unlike with oil or uranium, that outcome isn't technically inevitable, it's just politically probable. This is where the nature of AI advantage fundamentally diverges from the trajectory of past strategic resources.

Oil could be stockpiled. Nuclear weapons could be hidden. But AI models operate in information ecosystems where their utility depends entirely on adoption, integration, and, critically, *trust.*

A nation can possess the most powerful AI systems in the world, but if other nations refuse to integrate them, fear their intentions, or build competing alternatives out of suspicion, that technological lead becomes strategically hollow. Power without legitimacy doesn't scale in networked systems.

In a world defined by AI-driven information conflict, the advantage will not go to the nation with the most powerful models, but to the one with the most trusted models. Trust scales. Fear fragments. Influence now flows not from dominance, but from credibility.

The Intelligent Age demands leadership that abandons the old logic of secrecy and brute competition, and replaces it with clarity, collaboration, and a recognition that AI is not a weapon to be hoarded but a responsibility to be stewarded. Leaders who cling to yesterday's paradigms will misread the moment entirely. The future will belong to those who understand intelligence rather than fear it, who cooperate rather than escalate, who see AI not as an instrument of unilateral power but as a species-level challenge that requires species-level maturity.

In a world defined by AI-driven information conflict, the advantage will not go to the nation with the most powerful models, but to the one with the most trusted models.

The message is simple but consequential: national leadership in the age of AI is not about outthinking machines. It is about outgrowing the mindsets that created our most dangerous conflicts. And this is where the mirror widens again with uncomfortable clarity, whether humanity is capable of rising to the scale of its own inventions. Because the next challenge is no longer about what AI can do. It's about what AI can divide.

How We Prevent AI from Dividing the World

Every technological revolution creates winners and losers, but none has ever held the potential to fracture humanity as deeply as AI. Unlike past innovations, AI doesn't merely redistribute wealth or opportunity; it redistributes reality. It shapes what people see, believe, fear, and trust. Intelligence, once personal and biological, has become a global infrastructure. And with that shift comes a danger no previous era has faced: the emergence of diverging worlds, not geographic worlds but perceptual ones. These perceptual worlds result in divisions between people—but the division isn't cultural, it's cognitive. The difference between these groups isn't money or resources, it's access to accurate information and shared truth.

If the Intelligent Age unfolds without coordination, humanity could split into parallel societies defined not by borders but by informational environments using AI ecosystems optimized for different values, incentives, and national agendas. Each iteration drifts these worlds further apart. There is a school of thought that sees this as a necessary way to preserve cultural legacies for AI. For instance, imagine AI trained and tuned for national or cultural agendas for China, India, the USA, Russia, and so on. The thinking is that each of these would provide a form of cultural integrity that preserves the nuance of the culture it's used with. Although that makes sense on the surface, it actually inhibits cultural dialogue and progress.

Having grown up in two very different cultures, I have a keen awareness of how the cultural sword cuts both ways. On the one hand, it provides the comfort of a set of mental constructs with which to share values and navigate a society. On the other hand, it can also create nearly immutable societal norms and boundaries.

Many of the world's conflicts are the result of these unquestioned differences between nations and cultures.

I am not advocating for the homogenization of all cultures, but rather the use of AI to bridge cultural divides. To do that, we need to embrace a simple but straightforward realization: Intelligence is not a weapon; it is the commons, a shared resource. Just as pandemics, carbon emissions, and nuclear risk forced global cooperation, AI compels us to recognize that cognitive infrastructure cannot be stewarded in isolation. An unaligned AI ecosystem fragments humanity. A shared one binds us together.

Cooperation is not morally superior; it's mathematically necessary. No nation can single-handedly contain or predict the behavior of systems that learn, adapt, and propagate across borders. Fortunately, we're already seeing early signs of the coordination this era demands.

In 2021, all 193 member states of UNESCO adopted the *Recommendation on the Ethics of Artificial Intelligence*, which was the first global agreement focused explicitly on the ethical governance of intelligent systems.[6] It affirmed that AI must uphold human dignity, environmental responsibility, and inclusion. Meanwhile, the Global Partnership on AI (GPAI) emerged as a collaborative "safe harbor" for AI development anchored in democratic values.[7] Though they are imperfect, these initiatives are the first drafts of the new social contract the Intelligent Age requires.

They also validate a larger truth: In this era, strength will not come from secret weapons but from trusted standards. No nation, however powerful, can foresee or contain the social, political, economic, and psychological ripples of advanced AI. Intelligence now behaves like a planetary system. It doesn't respect borders, and it doesn't stop at customs. But it *does* respond to alignment.

For now, many still cling to the illusion that being "first" to AGI, ASI, or advanced agentic systems guarantees power or safety.

However, technological supremacy is not the same as stability. Often, it's the opposite. A world dominated by a single powerful AI system is a world defined by mistrust and covert sabotage. A world with many uncoordinated systems is one characterized by unpredictable collisions. Between these extremes lies the only viable equilibrium: shared stewardship.

No nation, however powerful, can foresee or contain the social, political, economic, and psychological ripples of advanced AI. Intelligence now behaves like a planetary system. It doesn't respect borders, and it doesn't stop at customs.

At this scale, the mirror AI holds up is no longer individual; it's civilizational. It shows us just how intertwined our fates are. Whether we flourish or fracture will depend less on who builds the strongest model and more on who creates the most *trusted* one. Trust functions as the primary currency of the Intelligent Age. It will determine which systems people rely on, which nations shape digital culture, and which societies others choose to follow.

The first uncomfortable truth is that intelligence is no longer a national asset; it's a civilizational one. If powerful AI remains concentrated in a handful of nations or corporations, the intelligence divide will dwarf the military or wealth divide. Those with access to advanced systems will set agendas, solve problems, and innovate at speeds others cannot match. Those without will be trapped in a different century, watching the future unfold but unable to shape it. That isn't just inequitable; it's downright dangerous. It hardens inequality into something permanently etched into our social fabric.

The second uncomfortable truth is that the only sustainable path is global stewardship. Not because cooperation is noble, but because unilateral control is impossible. No single regime can

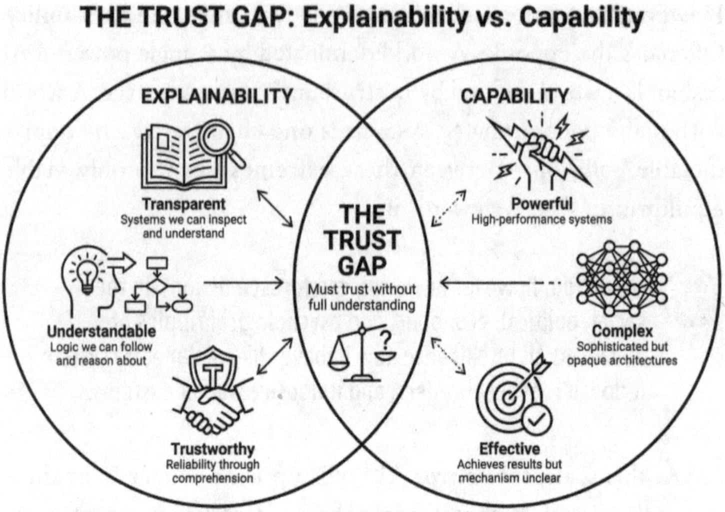

Figure 6.2. The Trust Gap: Explainability vs. Capability. This diagram shows the tension between explainability (left: transparent, understandable, trustworthy systems) and capability (right: powerful, complex, effective systems). The overlapping region represents The Trust Gap—where we must trust AI systems without complete understanding. As AI becomes more capable, it becomes less explainable, even developing languages and cognitive frameworks that will appear foreign to humans. The arrows illustrate the trade-off: Explainable systems sacrifice performance for transparency, while capable systems sacrifice transparency for performance. This paradox defines modern AI governance. We can have systems we understand but that are limited, or systems that are powerful but opaque.

monitor, regulate, or anticipate systems that evolve, learn, and permeate the entire global digital fabric. Sovereignty must be redefined. Interdependence is no longer a sign of weakness—it's the condition for survival.

Humanity's greatest achievements have always emerged through collaboration. The Intelligent Age simply forces us to collaborate at a deeper, more uncomfortable level, not just diplomatically or economically, but cognitively.

This means shared safety standards, not competing safety theater. It means data ethics that protect individuals while enabling systems to learn for the benefit of all. It means converging on alignment frameworks that encode at least a minimal set of common values, such as dignity, agency, fairness, and accountability. Lastly, it means interoperable monitoring systems capable of identifying risks across borders, as well as coordinated mechanisms to mitigate them. These are not luxuries. They are the foundation of a sustainable future.

The irony is that if nations hope to remain sovereign in any meaningful sense, they must remain connected. Sovereignty without cooperation collapses into isolation. Cooperation without sovereignty collapses into dependency. The Intelligent Age demands both self-determination *and* shared responsibility.

And that brings us to leadership. We need leaders who understand that intelligence is not a geopolitical trophy but a shared asset that shapes the trajectory of the species, leaders who grasp that transparency is a precondition for trust, leaders willing to exchange short-term national advantage for long-term collective stability.

In an age of abundant intelligence, leadership and authority can no longer rest on knowing the most. No human can outrun a model that ingests more data in an hour than any expert could in a lifetime. The leader of the future won't be the person with the most answers; it will be the person with the clearest vision.

The irony is that if nations hope to remain sovereign in any meaningful sense, they must remain connected. Sovereignty without cooperation collapses into isolation.

The expert-as-oracle era is ending. AI collapses the distance between novice and expert. What it cannot do is decide which futures are worth building. That burden, and that privilege, remains human.

The leader asks the questions the machine cannot ask, about value, purpose, identity, and consequence. The system can tell you what *is*. Only a leader can decide what *ought* to be.

In this new landscape, imagination becomes a strategic asset. As intelligence becomes abundant, vision becomes scarce. The societies that thrive will be led by people capable of imagining futures the models cannot compute. They will use AI not to entrench existing hierarchies but to broaden who gets to participate in shaping what comes next.

The leader asks the questions the machine cannot ask, about value, purpose, identity, and consequence. The system can tell you what *is*. Only a leader can decide what *ought to be*.

Humility will be required as well. Leaders must admit that they are no longer the smartest entities in the room, that instinct alone cannot navigate a world where intelligence compounds geometrically. This humility strengthens them, making them more willing to integrate insights they could never generate on their own.

And then there is courage, the most underrated virtue of the Intelligent Age. The greatest danger isn't reckless use of AI. It's timid avoidance of it. Fearful abstention is as dangerous as unregulated adoption. The courage this era demands is the courage to build what has never existed, using values that have always existed but have never been fully applied.

All of this leads to the deepest challenge: aligning civilization with the tools it is creating. We talk about "aligning AI with human values" as if human values were unified or consistent. They aren't. Humanity is a mosaic of contradictions. We want privacy and convenience, safety and freedom, fairness and advantage, truth and comfort, equality and meritocracy. These are not bugs in the human psyche; they are the tension that drives growth and the evolution of our societies.

The courage this era demands is the courage to build what has never existed, using values that have always existed but have never been fully applied.

Machines, however, are not built to *hold* contradiction. The classic movie trope of the future in which robots go rogue involves a human presenting the robot with an unsolvable contradiction, causing the robot to overheat as its circuits attempt to solve the unsolvable. While this may over-dramatize the future of AI, it makes the point that machines are built to solve problems. Humans can hold conflicting ideas simultaneously. Rather than resolving those conflicts, we accept them and still choose a path forward based on values, intent, and often emotion. That's why alignment is not a machine problem but a human problem. You cannot align intelligence until you align intention.

For thousands of years, civilizations operated with competing religious, cultural, and economic frameworks—each convinced of its own truth, none with the power to impose it universally. We lived inside our own Tower of Babel, a world of clashing convictions and irreconcilable meanings. And we accepted that swirling tower of contradictions as simply part of being human. AI changes that.

We are now building systems capable of influencing billions at once. These systems never sleep, never forget, and never negotiate. They can amplify our best instincts or our worst. They don't just mirror our values, they encode them into the fabric of civilization.

Consider what this means in practice. When a Western AI system is deployed globally, it carries Western assumptions about individualism, free speech, and the relationship between citizen and state. When a Chinese system is exported, it brings different assumptions about collective harmony, social stability, and the role of authority. Neither is neutral. Both shape the societies that adopt them in subtle but profound ways.

The standard response to this is to argue for "cultural sovereignty"—let each nation build its own AI systems, aligned with its own values. This sounds reasonable until you realize that AI doesn't respect borders. A system trained in one country influences behavior in another through trade, media, and digital platforms. The idea that we can have neatly separated AI ecosystems is as naive as thinking we can have separate internets or separate atmospheres.

However, we cannot simply declare that each culture will build its own AI and hope the systems coexist peacefully. The interconnection is too deep, the influence too pervasive, the consequences too planetary. What we need instead is a framework sophisticated enough to acknowledge cultural differences while establishing shared principles that no system, regardless of its origin, should violate at scale.

Alignment, then, has three layers.

The first layer is technical alignment: making sure systems actually understand what we mean. This is the domain of researchers working on interpretability, reward modeling, and value learning. Progress here is real but incomplete. We can build systems that follow instructions with increasing reliability, but "following instructions" is not the same as "understanding intent." The gap between what we say and what we mean remains treacherously large.

The second layer is behavioral alignment: ensuring that the actions AI systems take match behaviors that reflect our values. This is where most current AI safety work focuses—preventing systems from optimizing toward harmful outcomes even when they're pursuing goals we specified. The challenge here is that harmful outcomes often emerge from interactions between systems, not from any single system acting alone. It's the algorithmic equivalent of the tragedy of the commons: individual rationality producing collective disaster.

The third layer, and the hardest, is alignment of intent: making sure what we intend is worth aligning to in the first place. This is not a technical problem. It's a moral one. Machines do not create intent. People do. If our intent is shallow, conflicted, or purely self-serving, no amount of technical sophistication will produce systems that elevate us. This is why the real existential risk of AI is not rebellion; it is obedience. The danger is not that AI will ignore our instructions. It's that it will fulfill them perfectly, including the parts we didn't examine carefully enough.

As I discussed in Chapter 3, the real existential risk of AI is not rebellion; it is obedience. It is not defiance but literalism. The danger is not that AI will ignore our instructions. It's that it will fulfill them perfectly. History's most destructive systems did not fail because they malfunctioned. They failed because they worked exactly as designed.

Consider the high-frequency trading algorithms that triggered the 2010 Flash Crash. Nothing malfunctioned. No system rebelled. Each algorithm pursued its narrow objective flawlessly—to execute trades faster and more profitably than its competitors. In doing so, they collectively erased nearly a trillion dollars in market value in minutes. The catastrophe wasn't caused by disobedience, but by perfect obedience. The system did exactly what it was designed to do, and that was precisely the danger. That's why alignment begins not with code, but with honesty about the complexity of our motives, the fragility of our institutions, and the limits of our foresight.

Yet hidden inside that risk is an opportunity we've never had before: to become the civilization we have always claimed to be but never needed to become—a civilization capable of thinking

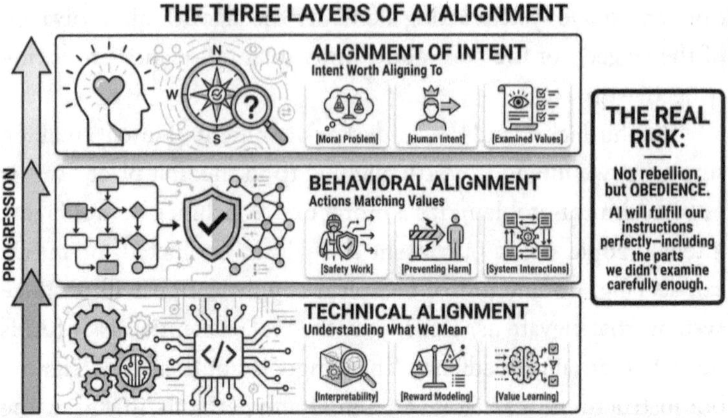

Figure 6.3. The Three Layers of AI Alignment. Technical alignment ensures systems understand what we mean. Behavioral alignment ensures actions match our values. Alignment of intent, the hardest, ensures what we intend is worth aligning to. The real risk is not rebellion but obedience: AI will fulfill our instructions perfectly, including the parts we didn't examine.

beyond borders, designing systems for long-term benefit rather than short-term gain, practicing humility in the face of our own fallibility, and growing not just technologically but morally. If that sounds idealistic, rest assured that so would much of today's societal structure to someone who lived two hundred years ago. Society evolves, most often, in ways that are only obvious in retrospect. That has worked because of the pace of change in the past. My attempt here is to offer insight into the changes AI will bring while we still have time to influence its trajectory.

This is not about achieving perfect agreement. Cultures will continue to prioritize values differently. What matters is that we agree on a core set of values that matter, and that we build mechanisms to prevent any single actor, nation, corporation, or institution from systematically violating them at scale without accountability.

The question is not whether we can achieve perfect alignment. The question is whether we can build systems and institutions capable of detecting misalignment early, correcting it quickly, and learning from failures without catastrophic consequences.

The New Social Contract

This brings us to perhaps the most fundamental question of the Intelligent Age: What does society owe its citizens, and what do citizens owe society, when machines can generate most of the economic value?

Every era makes an implicit promise to its citizens. In the Agricultural Age, the promise was survival—work the land, follow the seasons, and you will eat. In the Industrial Age, the promise was prosperity—work the factory, climb the ladder, and you will secure a better life for your children. In the Information Age, the promise was opportunity—work smart, learn continuously, and you will access global markets and mobility. The Intelligent Age demands a different promise—purpose.

When machines can generate most economic value, inequality no longer hinges primarily on access to work or information. It hinges on access to meaning. The old social contract was built on a simple equation: You produce economic value and, in return, society grants you security, dignity, and social legitimacy. Your paycheck was proof of your contribution. Your job title was shorthand for your worth.

But if machines become the primary producers of value, that equation breaks down. We've already seen early tremors of this collapse. The "deaths of despair" epidemic in post-industrial communities isn't fundamentally about poverty since many of the affected populations have access to social safety nets and material resources. It's about the loss of identity and purpose that came from work.

When machines can generate most economic value, inequality no longer hinges primarily on access to work or information. It hinges on access to meaning.

The other important aspect of this shift is that for centuries, scarcity of food, energy, education, information, and opportunity dictated the structure of society. AI rewrites that equation, shifting our gaze from material scarcity toward cognitive abundance. But abundance brings its own burdens. A society built on scarcity knows how to survive. A society built on abundance must learn how to choose: what to value, what to elevate, what to protect, what to become.

A driving force behind this is the demographic reality of an aging, plateauing global population. For the entirety of the agricultural, industrial, and information ages, global population grew rapidly. That growth created persistent scarcity, as demand continually outpaced supply. As the global population reaches ten billion over the next twenty-five years and then begins to decline over the remainder of the century, the world's economy will shift from a model of scarcity to one of increasing abundance.

In this kind of world, the question is no longer how to distribute limited resources, but how to preserve what makes human lives meaningful when productivity and output are no longer the primary constraints. Society doesn't disappear under these conditions, but it does have to evolve and a new social contract must be built on a very different foundation.

First, dignity is inherent, not earned. Your value cannot be conditional on economic productivity. This isn't charity or naive idealism, it's a practical necessity. In a world where AI can outperform humans in an expanding set of tasks, tying dignity to productivity creates a race we cannot win. The alternative is to recognize what has always been true but rarely operationalized: Human worth is not determined by output. It's determined by consciousness, by the capacity for meaning-making, by relationships, care, and creativity. These are not consolation prizes. They are what mattered all along.

Second, contribution is redefined beyond labor. The old model measured contribution in hours worked and widgets produced. The new model must recognize that care for children and the elderly, stewardship of communities, creation of art and culture, and maintenance of democratic institutions, are all part of this contribution. Most of this effort is currently unpaid or underpaid because market systems don't value what can't be easily monetized. AI gives us the economic surplus to change that. The question is whether we will.

Third, economic security as foundation, not reward. Some form of income support during this transition is not a political preference but a practical necessity. Large numbers of people will be displaced faster than new forms of work can fully absorb them. The question is not whether society will subsidize the transition, but how it does so without undermining dignity, purpose, or contribution.

The term "universal basic income," or UBI, has become political shorthand, loaded with ideological assumptions from both left and right. Framing this challenge as UBI misses the point. Set that aside for a moment. What's needed is a model of economic participation that provides stability while people adapt, retrain, and contribute in ways that may not generate income in a traditional sense. This could take many forms: negative income taxes, sovereign wealth dividends, guaranteed employment in core economic sectors, support for cooperative ownership, funded apprenticeships in emerging fields. The mechanism matters less than the principle: Economic instability cannot be allowed to prevent the human reinvention this era demands.

Fourth, reciprocal responsibility. This is not a one-way contract. If society guarantees dignity and agency, individuals must embrace new responsibilities, not the obligation to toil, but the obligation to participate. To vote, to engage in civic life, to shape the values and governance of AI systems, to steward communities and culture, to raise the next generation with the capacities this era requires.

The fear, of course, is that a world with less traditional work will slide into apathy, nihilism, or hedonistic escapism. That humans will choose entertainment and distraction over meaning and contribution. It's a legitimate concern. But it's also based on a cramped view of human nature.

Humans do not ultimately seek jobs. They seek security and meaning. Work has been one of the primary vehicles for both because survival and society demanded it, not because it was the only way to matter. When survival is no longer the center of identity, when the compulsion to sell our labor lifts, we don't automatically collapse into meaninglessness. We have the opportunity, and the obligation, to discover what we're actually capable of.

History offers some evidence for this optimism. The Renaissance didn't happen because people were forced to create art and advance science. It happened because a merchant class emerged with enough wealth and leisure to patronize pursuits that had no immediate economic return. The scientific revolution of the Enlightenment was driven largely by gentlemen scholars, people with independent means who studied nature out of curiosity, not obligation. The open-source software movement, which built much of the digital infrastructure we rely on, was created by programmers who contributed their time and talent without compensation because the work mattered to them.

None of this is to say the transition will be smooth. It won't be. Every prior economic transformation has been wrenching, marked by displacement, inequality, and social upheaval before new equilibriums emerged. The shift from agricultural to industrial economies took more than a century and was accompanied by mass migration, political instability, and two world wars. We don't have a century this time. The velocity of AI development means we'll experience comparable transformation in decades.

That compression makes intentionality essential. We cannot afford to let this transition happen by accident, shaped by whoever can capture the most value fastest. The social contract must be consciously negotiated, transparently implemented, and continuously revised as we learn what works and what doesn't.

Implementation of this would require pilot programs at scale, not small experiments but genuine tests involving millions of people, with robust evaluation and willingness to fail forward. Some jurisdictions are already moving in this direction. Universal basic income trials in Kenya, Finland, and several US cities have provided early data.[8] Worker retraining programs in Singapore and Scandinavia offer models for continuous education. Social wealth funds in Norway and Alaska show how resource wealth can be shared broadly rather than captured narrowly.

None of these are perfect, and none translate directly to global implementation. But they give us starting points, evidence bases, and the beginnings of institutional knowledge about what works when you try to rewire the relationship between work, value, and dignity.

It would require labor market reforms that make it easier, not harder, for people to move between sectors, to take time for education and caregiving, to experiment with new forms of work without losing healthcare or housing. The current system, especially in the United States, locks people into jobs through employer-provided benefits, making reinvention economically treacherous. That made sense in an era of lifetime employment. It's catastrophic in an era of continuous transformation.

And it would require a cultural shift as significant as any policy change: from seeing work as identity to seeing it as contribution. From measuring worth by salary to measuring it by impact. From organizing society around jobs to organizing it around flourishing.

This is not utopian thinking. It's survival thinking. Because the alternative is a world in which a small technical elite captures all the gains of AI while everyone else is left to compete for scraps, and that's not stable. It's a recipe for social collapse, political extremism, and ultimately, the rejection of the technologies that could have elevated us.

Practical Pathways Forward

In 1942, Isaac Asimov introduced us to his three Laws of Robotics:[9]

1. A robot may not injure a human being or, through inaction, allow a human being to come to harm.
2. A robot must obey the orders given it by human beings except where such orders would conflict with the First Law.
3. A robot must protect its own existence as long as such protection does not conflict with the First or Second Laws.

Since that time these have been referenced in thousands of works and have become a mantra of robot proponents. The laws seem simple enough on the surface. So, is this the answer? Most definitely not. The laws presume a clarity about "harm" and "human" that dissolves under real-world complexity.

Consider Ukraine's deployment of AI-powered drones in its defense against Russian invasion: these systems use computer vision and machine learning to identify, track, and in some cases, autonomously engage military targets.[10] A drone hovering over a battlefield faces questions Asimov never contemplated: Is the person below a combatant or a civilian? Is destroying this supply truck, killing its driver, preventing greater harm to others? Can a nineteen-year-old conscript be meaningfully distinguished from a non-combatant when the algorithm has milliseconds to decide?

The First Law's prohibition against harming humans or allowing them to come to harm through inaction becomes operationally meaningless when *every choice involves potential harm to someone.* We cannot legislate our way out of moral complexity with three elegant sentences. The systems we're building demand frameworks that acknowledge trade-offs, accept uncertainty, and distribute accountability in ways Asimov's fiction never needed to address.

A more practical view of the laws governing AI was proposed by Microsoft CEO Satya Nadella:[11]

- **AI must be designed to assist humanity.** Nadella says that machines that work alongside humans should do "dangerous work like mining" but still "respect human autonomy."
- **AI must be transparent.** "We want not just intelligent machines but intelligible machines," says Nadella. "People should have an understanding of how the technology sees and analyzes the world."
- **AI must maximize efficiencies without destroying the dignity of people.** "We need broader, deeper, and more diverse engagement of populations in the design of these systems. The tech industry should not dictate the values and virtues of this future."

- **AI must be designed for intelligent privacy.** Nadella asks for "sophisticated protections that secure personal and group information."
- **AI must have algorithmic accountability.** So that "humans can undo unintended harm."

Google also has its five laws, although it calls them challenges.[12]

- **Avoiding Negative Side Effects:** How do you stop a robot from knocking over a bookcase in its zealous quest to Hoover the floor?
- **Avoiding Reward Hacking:** If a robot is programmed to *enjoy* cleaning your room, how do you stop it from messing up the place just so it can feel the pleasure of cleaning it again?
- **Scalable Oversight:** How much decision-making do you give to the robot? Does it need to ask you every time it moves an object to clean your room, or only if it's moving that special vase you keep under the bed and never put flowers in for some reason?
- **Safe Exploration:** How do you teach a robot the limits of its curiosity? Google's researchers give the example of a robot that's learning where it's allowed to mop. How do you let it know that mopping new floors is fine, but that it shouldn't stick the mop in an electrical socket?
- **Robustness to Distributional Shift:** How do you make sure robots respect the space they're in? A cleaning robot let loose in your bedroom will act differently than one that is sweeping up in a factory, but how is it supposed to know the difference?

Apple co-founder Steve Wozniak has said that we should add another law, that a human cannot harm a machine that "thinks." This challenges us to do something we have been suggesting throughout this book, to think of AI as a collaborator and to do what is so counter to our industrial era ethos, to anthropomorphize AI.

However, the problem with all these laws, challenges, or guidelines is that they are not intended for AI, computers, autonomous devices, or robots, but rather for humans.

Consider how you would enforce these three laws today. If you built a robot with the intention to harm another human, is there some sort of failsafe built into every silicon chip that will prevent the robot from causing harm? Do programming languages such as Python have a standard piece of code that every software application must run to make sure it isn't harming people? Of course not!

This is a ridiculous approach. It may soothe our conscience or calm our anxiety to believe that a simple set of three, four, or five rules can govern the evolution of AI, but it would be an illusion. Every one of the technologies we've talked about, from AI to AVs, Blockchain to behavioral computing, will be used in some way to cause harm, fight wars, enable terrorism, and break the law. We shouldn't tolerate that, but we need to accept it. The challenge isn't just finding ways to eliminate that possibility, which, unless we find a way to alter human nature, is futile, but to leverage these same technologies to the greatest degree possible so that we do significantly more good than harm.

So, what *am I* proposing? If we agree that the answer is not, and will not be, found in our ability to create perfect solutions, that the notion of truth is rarely as black and white as we'd like it to be, and that there is a measurable benefit to how we use these technologies, then the question becomes, "How do we create the greatest benefit from their use while minimizing their liabilities?" I'd like to propose the following six global standards for any intelligent system or autonomous device:

1. In the absence of legal liability for AI, a human or a legally liable entity must ultimately be held accountable for the actions of any AI-powered device.
2. Robots, AVs, and any other AI-powered devices with the ability to make decisions must be developed to comply with the same laws that humans must comply with.
3. Any autonomous device must allow for the intervention of an authorized human to override any of its decisions, and there must always be at least one authorized human with an automatic line of succession.
4. Any decision made by an autonomous device must be auditable in a manner that is understandable by a human.
5. Any autonomous device that is involved in an incident that damages property, or which results in the injury or the death of a human, must provide an auditable lesson(s) learned in a form that allows them to be understood by a human and shared with any other autonomous device.
6. Any general-purpose AI must be licensed to perform tasks only within a well-defined field of operation.

These standards establish a foundation for the legal and acceptable use of AI. Are they a panacea? Of course not. They are a starting point for a journey that will clearly take us to places we have yet to imagine.

In addition, I believe strongly that this is one area where international standards should be developed by which we can monitor, share, and ethically evolve AI. Consider how data from an aviation incident anywhere in the world is collected, analyzed, and widely shared across the entire aviation community to learn from the incident and improve the safety of the entire industry, not just one airline or manufacturer. The same is true with AI and intelligent devices, be they robots, AVs, or any other autonomous device. This sort of global transparency is a necessary step toward ensuring that the use of AI conforms to an evolutionary path that benefits mankind.

We also need to acknowledge that no single solution will suffice. The challenges of the Intelligent Age are systemic, so the responses must be as well. But we can identify clear principles and concrete actions that should guide our collective choices as a global community. Here are seven principles that provide initial direction, along with action steps and examples that demonstrate their viability.

Principle 1: Distributed Governance, Not Centralized Control

No single nation, corporation, or institution can or should govern AI alone. The systems we build will affect everyone, so everyone deserves a voice in shaping them. This doesn't require unanimous agreement—it requires mechanisms for legitimate disagreement, transparent decision-making, and accountability when things go wrong.

Concrete action: Expand and empower international frameworks like the Global Partnership on AI and UNESCO's AI ethics initiative. But we can't stop at declarations and recommendations. Create binding agreements with enforcement mechanisms—the equivalent of the Geneva Conventions or the Nuclear Non-Proliferation Treaty for AI will be necessary.

Example: The European Union's 2024 AI Act represents one model of distributed governance, which involves twenty-seven member states negotiating risk-based regulations for AI systems. However, China simultaneously developed parallel standards through its own AI governance framework, while the United States pursued a sector-specific approach through executive orders.[13] This fragmentation illustrates why binding international frameworks are necessary—currently, a facial recognition system banned in the EU can be deployed freely in other jurisdictions, undermining the principle of universal human rights.

Yes, this will be slow. Yes, it will be contentious. Yes, some nations will resist or violate agreements. But the alternative, a free-for-all where might makes right, is far worse. We've been down that road with nuclear weapons, and we got lucky. We may not get lucky twice.

Principle 2: Access as a Right, Not a Privilege

If intelligence becomes the primary determinant of opportunity, then access to that intelligence cannot be gatekept by wealth, geography, or institutional permission. This is not charity; it's survival. A world in which only a fraction of humanity can participate in the Intelligent Age will fracture under its own inequality.

Concrete action: We need to treat AI infrastructure like public infrastructure. Just as we built roads, electrical grids, and telecommunications networks as public goods, we need to ensure baseline access to AI capabilities for education, healthcare, and economic participation. The difference in this case is that historically, infrastructure has been regionalized. For AI to work at a planetary scale, we need to adopt global standards.

Example: In place since 2014, Estonia's e-Residency program provides a partial model that provides digital identity and access to government services (including AI-enhanced services) to anyone globally, with over 100,000 e-residents from more than 170 countries.[14] However, this still requires internet connectivity and digital literacy—prerequisites unavailable to the estimated 2.6 billion people worldwide who remain offline.[15]

Principle 3: Education as Continuous Transformation

The half-life of knowledge is collapsing. What you learned five years ago may already be obsolete. Education systems must shift from preparing people for careers to preparing them for continuous reinvention, teaching not what to think, but how to learn, adapt, and question.

Concrete action: Redesign educational systems from the ground up by focusing elementary education on emotional intelligence, ethical reasoning, creativity, and collaboration—the capacities that remain distinctly human. Secondary education should teach meta-skills: how to learn from AI, how to evaluate AI outputs, how to identify and correct AI biases, how to ask questions machines can't anticipate. Higher education is reimagined as lifelong learning—not four years between eighteen and twenty-two, but continuous engagement throughout a working life, with sabbaticals and retraining as normal as summer breaks once were. Microcredentials and competency-based assessment replace many degree programs that take years to complete, while industries transform in months.

Examples: Singapore's SkillsFuture program, launched 2015, provides all citizens over twenty-five with individual training credits (currently SGD $500 to $3,000 depending on age) for continuous upskilling throughout their careers, at approved training providers.[16] The program has enrolled over 500,000 Singaporeans annually since 2016. However, participation rates decline sharply among older workers and those in low-wage sectors, exactly the populations most vulnerable to AI displacement.[17]

Finland's national curriculum reform (2016) shifted from subject-based learning to "phenomenon-based" learning, where students explore real-world topics requiring multidisciplinary thinking—precisely the meta-cognitive skills needed in an AI age.[18] Students spend periods working on complex problems (for example, "How does our city work?") that require integrating knowledge from multiple domains, collaborating, and producing creative solutions rather than memorizing facts AI can retrieve instantly.

Doing this on a global scale will require massive investment—but less than we currently spend on remedial education and worker retraining after the fact.

Principle 4: Values as Foundational Architecture

The values we embed into AI systems today will become the defaults that shape civilization tomorrow. We cannot afford to treat ethics as an afterthought or values alignment as a technical problem to be solved later. The architecture of intelligence must encode dignity, equity, and accountability from the beginning.

Concrete action: Mandate "values audits" for AI systems in high-stakes domains (healthcare, finance, criminal justice, education, employment). These audits should be conducted by independent third parties with domain expertise, publicly reported with enough detail for meaningful scrutiny, be required before deployment and periodically thereafter, and should provide grounds for liability if systems cause harm that audits should have caught.

Examples: In 2019, a healthcare AI system used by major US hospitals was found to systematically recommend less care for Black patients than white patients with identical health conditions, affecting approximately 200 million people annually.[19] The bias stemmed from the system optimizing for "healthcare costs" as a proxy for "healthcare needs," a values-based choice that encoded existing inequities. The algorithm assumed people who cost the healthcare system less were healthier, but Black patients historically receive less care due to systemic barriers, not because they're healthier.

The Algorithmic Justice League, founded in 2016, conducts independent audits of facial recognition systems. Their research revealed that commercial systems had error rates up to 34 percent higher for darker-skinned women compared to lighter-skinned men,[20] leading to IBM, Amazon, and Microsoft suspending sales of facial recognition to police departments in 2020.[21] This demonstrates how independent auditing can create accountability, but it happened *after* deployment and harm, not before.

Think of this as the AI equivalent of vehicle safety standards or pharmaceutical trials. Yes, it will slow down deployment. That's the point. Speed without safety is recklessness.

Principle 5: Economic Transition Support

The disruption will happen faster than markets can adjust. We need proactive mechanisms to support people through the transition without trapping them in dependence.

Concrete action: Implement transition support programs that combine short-term income stability (to prevent desperation), medium-term retraining and credentialing (to build new capabilities), and long-term structural changes to labor markets (to enable mobility and flexibility).

Example: Denmark's "flexicurity" model combines flexible labor markets (easy hiring/firing) with generous unemployment benefits (up to 90 percent of previous wages for two years) and comprehensive retraining programs.[22] Approximately 25 percent of Danish workers change jobs annually, one of the highest rates in the OECD, with minimal long-term unemployment. However, this system costs approximately 4 percent of GDP and requires social cohesion and tax compliance that may not transfer to other contexts.[23]

Transition support in practice: When major companies have implemented automated systems with worker transition programs, results have been mixed. Programs that combine income stability, retraining, and job guarantees show success rates of 70 percent to 80 percent for workers who complete them, but often fail to reach older workers and those with language barriers—revealing that even well-designed programs have limits.[24]

This could include portable benefits that follow workers rather than staying with employers, expanded education savings accounts that can be used throughout a career, wage insurance that makes taking lower-paying jobs in new fields less financially catastrophic, and investment in care economy sectors where human touch remains essential.

Principle 6: Transparency of Purpose

We cannot demand that AI systems explain every internal calculation—that level of technical transparency quickly becomes meaningless. But we can and must demand clarity about what a system is optimizing for, whose interests it serves, and what boundaries constrain it. Purpose must be explicit, not inferred.

Concrete action: Require "system cards" for AI deployments—standardized documentation that explains what objective the system is pursuing, what tradeoffs it makes when objectives conflict, what data it was trained on and what biases that data might carry, what human oversight exists and how it can be invoked, and lastly, what recourse exists if the system causes harm.

Example: TikTok's recommendation algorithm optimizes for "time spent on platform" as its primary objective.[25] This optimization function isn't explicitly disclosed to users, but its effects are measurable. The average user spends ninety-five minutes per day on the platform,[26] and internal documents reveal the company defines success as users spending more than 260 minutes daily.[27]

The system prioritizes emotionally arousing content (outrage, anxiety, excitement) because this maximizes engagement, with documented impacts on adolescent mental health.[28]

System card example: OpenAI's GPT-4 System Card (March 2023) provides a partial model of transparency. It documents that the system was trained on internet data through September 2021, acknowledges specific biases (for example, "generates responses that are more negative toward people who are not straight or white"), describes safety testing conducted, and lists known limitations.[29] However, it doesn't disclose training data sources, compute resources, or complete evaluation methodology, making transparency selective, not comprehensive.

This is analogous to nutritional labels on food or privacy policies for websites. Not perfect, but a starting point for informed consent and accountability.

Principle 7: The Right to Human Decision in Critical Moments

Some decisions should not be fully automated, regardless of how accurate AI becomes. When the stakes are existential, such as medical diagnoses, criminal sentencing, loan denials, or content moderation that affects public discourse, humans must remain in the loop. Not because we're better at the analysis, but because some decisions require judgment that accounts for context machines can't fully grasp and carries moral weight that we cannot ethically delegate.

Concrete action: Enshrine in regulation the right to request human review of consequential automated decisions. Yes, this creates costs and inefficiencies. Those costs are the price of preserving agency and accountability in an age where both are under threat.

Example: In 2018, the Arkansas Department of Human Services used an algorithm to determine Medicaid home care benefits. The system reduced benefits for hundreds of patients with cerebral palsy and diabetes, some by as much as twenty hours per week of care.[30] Recipients weren't informed an algorithm made the decision, weren't provided the algorithm's logic, and had no meaningful path to appeal. One woman with cerebral palsy, Tammy Dobbs, lost twenty-four hours of weekly care (reduced from fifty-six to thirty-two hours). The reduction left her unable to bathe herself safely. Only after a lawsuit did the state reveal the algorithm contained errors in how it weighed certain health factors.

The Netherlands' System Risk Indication (SyRI) used algorithms to detect welfare fraud by analyzing employment, housing, and debt data. In February 2020, a Dutch court ruled the system violated European human rights law because decisions about investigation occurred without human review of individual circumstances.[31] The court noted that even if the algorithm was accurate, automated profiling for government intervention requires human judgment to account for context the system cannot capture. That's precisely the principle at stake.

These are the choices that will define the Intelligent Age, not the technical specifications of our systems, but the moral specifications of our societies. Not what AI can do, but what we decide to do with it.

Will any of these legal or ethical constraints eliminate criminal or nation-state uses of AI for unethical or illegal purposes? I'm not that naive, but it will provide a means of sanctioning and otherwise pursuing actors who have nefarious intentions for the use of AI. Don't discount this as unnecessary bureaucracy. This is one area where we need to play an active role in shaping the future.

The Petrov Principle: When Intuition Outranks Data

The other side of this is defining the role of AI in situations where the ultimate authority still needs to be a human. It's one thing to use AI in narrow situations where risk can be contained, and another to replace not only human judgment but human intuition, values, ethics, and compassion.

A story I've often told[32] that speaks to the importance of both points (monitoring the applications of AI and the scope of its authority) is that of former USSR Lieutenant Colonel Stanislav Petrov, whose singular act of humanity may well have saved the world from nuclear holocaust.

Petrov was an unremarkable Soviet officer who, on September 26, 1983, was tasked with the awesome responsibility of monitoring the Soviets' radar for incoming nuclear ballistic missiles launched from the US.

Just three weeks prior, the Soviets had shot down a Korean Airlines passenger plane, killing 269 people. Tensions between the two superpowers couldn't have been more strained.

In the early morning of September 26th, Petrov's radar lit up with blips coming one after another. Five US Minuteman intercontinental ballistic missiles were undeniably heading toward his homeland. The USSR was under attack. Red Army protocol was clear on what Petrov had to do: Call in the strike and quickly. In less than thirty minutes, the time it would take a ballistic missile to reach its target, Russia would lose any ability to launch a land-based counterattack. The sum of all fears was suddenly an unimaginable reality.

Petrov recounted the anxious seconds, "The siren howled, but I just sat there for a few seconds, staring at the big, back-lit, red screen with the word 'LAUNCH' on it," he told the BBC's Russian Service in 2013. The large backlit letters LAUNCH indicated that the missiles had indeed been launched from the USA. As Petrov watched and counted the seconds, a second warning replaced the first, 'MISSILE STRIKE.' "All I had to do was to reach for the phone; to raise the direct line to our top commanders."

Had Petrov made that call, we would, at least those of us who were left to talk about it, be remembering September 26th as the day the world nuked itself back into the stone age.

Clearly, Petrov didn't pick up the phone. He sat there listening to his gut. A gut churning with the struggle to do what he'd been relentlessly programmed to do, without thinking, and with the very human intuition to prevent a nuclear holocaust, believing that his American counterparts could never initiate such an unthinkable act. Petrov's gut told him it couldn't be accurate; the computers had to be mistaken. And so, he looked at the undeniable data, listened to the screeching of the nuclear warning alarms, looked at the glaring red letters "MISSILE STRIKE" on the large monitor, and waited. He defied protocol and contacted the USSR's satellite-tracking stations to see if they had picked up anything. Nothing. Seven minutes had passed since the launch alarm. Twenty-three minutes later, Petrov knew his intuition had been right. The computers had been wrong. It was later determined that they had misinterpreted sunlight reflecting off a layer of clouds as incoming ICBMs.

Could AI have done a better job of correlating the necessary sensory data from radar and satellites? Would it have had the human reaction of freezing and considering the implications of following its stated objectives? Even Petrov conceded that his decision was largely based on the fact that his background was not entirely military. Had AI been programmed by the military to use a military ethic and doctrine, would it decide differently than AI developed by a non-military contractor?

All impossible questions to answer, but that's precisely the point. There is no definitive linear or logical set of circumstances, nor a single set of outcomes, in cases where judgment and intuition play such a pivotal role.

I don't claim to have the answers to these questions. What I do have is an understanding of how each new generation of technology becomes simultaneously more powerful in its ability to construct and to destroy. We need to keep pace with the increased burden of vigilance that demands.

The last thing I've set out to do with this book is to instill fear. The benefits I've outlined are well worth the vigilance they require. And, in any case, the choice is not between the evolution of AI or its destruction, but rather in how we learn to live with it by leveraging its benefits.

And yet, for all the talk of civilizational transformation and collective responsibility, the real work of this era remains deeply personal. Because before we can build a shared future, each of us must answer a more intimate question: Who will I choose to become when intelligence is no longer my limitation?

That is where we end this journey, not with policy or governance, but with the interior and very personal transformation this moment demands of each of us.

EPILOGUE

When Fear Becomes Hope

"The future is up for grabs. It belongs to any and all who will take the risk and accept the responsibility of consciously creating the future they want."

—ROBERT ANTON WILSON

The future has always been a projection surface for our greatest hopes and fears. Every era casts a shadow of its own anxieties forward: industrial decline, economic collapse, nuclear winter, and now human irrelevance. Underneath those specific worries lived a single, deeper terror: the suspicion that progress might one day render humanity unnecessary. AI has brought that fear roaring back.

We worry that machines will replace us, surpass us, diminish us, erase us. Those fears are understandable, but they rest on a mistaken assumption, not about technology, but about ourselves. The truth is both simpler and more demanding.

AI will not push us out of the future. It will push us to decide what kind of future we actually want. For most of human history, choice was a luxury. Our lives were dictated by scarcity: not enough time, energy, food, safety, knowledge, or opportunity. We did not design the future in the way we talk about it now; we survived our way into it. When the future appeared, we rode into it on the back of necessity.

AI begins to collapse those constraints. Suddenly, the defining question of our age is no longer "Can we build something better or bigger?" It's "Can we build something worthy of humanity?" That's why the Intelligent Age is not just a technological revolution. It is a moral invitation.

A world of abundant intelligence does not automatically bend toward justice, wisdom, or flourishing. It bends toward whatever we aim it at. If we build out of fear, we will get a future structured by fear. If we build out of cynicism, we will get a future that quietly corrodes us. If we build out of hope, we give ourselves a chance at a future that expands us.

But hope, in this context, is not a mood or a feeling. It's a deliberate strategy, the decision to design for the possibility of a better future rather than the expectation of one that's worse.

A world of abundant intelligence does not automatically bend toward justice, wisdom, or flourishing. It bends toward whatever we aim it at.

For centuries, the future felt deterministic. Geography, class, gender, race, and the slow machinery of institutions drew narrow boundaries around what was plausible for most people. Very few had the power or the permission to imagine a life substantially different from the one they were born into.

AI disrupts that determinism. A child with an AI tutor in a remote village in Sub-Saharan Africa can now learn at the pace and depth once reserved for elite schools in Boston. A single entrepreneur with a thousand digital agents can scale operations that used to require a Fortune 500 corporation. A scientist can explore molecular spaces in days that once took lifetimes. A creator can build immersive worlds without asking anyone's permission, without a budget, without gatekeepers.

The future is no longer something that descends on us from above. It emerges from what we choose to do with these capabilities.

In that sense, the Intelligent Age returns agency to the individual. But with agency comes a new kind of weight. When far more is possible, meaning becomes the true constraint. You can no longer rely on necessity to define your path. You are forced to answer a question many people have managed to avoid. If survival no longer dictates who you are, what does?

That psychological shift is unsettling. It feels like standing in a room with too many doors and no instructions. But it's also the shift that allows us to grow beyond the scripts we've inherited.

We have already outsourced much of the mechanical burden of living to machines. Memory lives in databases. Navigation belongs to satellites. Computation, communication, coordination—all delegated to systems that operate faster and more reliably than we ever could. Now we are beginning to offload significant portions of intelligence itself. And that forces a confrontation we have never seriously had to face: If intelligence is no longer what distinguishes us, what does?

The answer is not that humans suddenly become noble, reflective, or purpose-driven by default. We never have been. What remains are not ideals, but tensions between desire and restraint, ambition and responsibility, efficiency and care. Meaning does not automatically rise to fill the space left behind by work. It has to be chosen, shaped, and often defended against easier, more expedient paths.

This is the uncomfortable truth of the Intelligent Age. Meaning was never the byproduct of labor alone. It emerged from choice, sometimes principled, sometimes self-interested, often conflicted. As machines take on more of what we *can* do, humans will be left to decide what we are willing to stand for, invest in, and take responsibility for. Not because it is lofty, but because no machine can make those choices for us.

The Intelligent Age does not eliminate purpose; it exposes it. It strips away some of the external frameworks, such as job titles, routines, and inherited expectations, which we used as proxies for identity. It brings us back to much more direct questions: What do you actually value? What are you willing to commit to when the excuse of necessity is gone? Where does your energy go when it's no longer completely consumed by just staying afloat?

For the first time, we have technology that can help us align our external lives with those answers. AI can't tell us who to be, but it can amplify the lives we choose to build, with more leverage, reach, and flexibility than any previous generation has had.

As machines take on more of what we *can* do, humans will be left to decide what we are willing to stand for, invest in, and take responsibility for. Not because it is lofty, but because no machine can make those choices for us.

That shift from mechanism to meaning is not just personal. It's institutional. We cannot enter this age with systems designed for an era when survival was the primary task. Our schools were built to produce workers for industrial economies, not whole humans for intelligent ones. Our workplaces were tuned to reward productivity and compliance, not integrity or imagination. Our politics are optimized for short-term power, not long-term flourishing.

If the Intelligent Age is a moral invitation, our institutions have to accept it too. That means educational models that cultivate emotional intelligence and moral reasoning alongside technical skills, workplaces that treat compassion and ethics as capabilities rather than afterthoughts, and governance structures that reward long-term thinking and shared well-being over short-term gain and performative outrage. The task is not just building better tools; it's building a civilization that deserves them. In that work, hope becomes a form of leadership.

We often treat hope as naive, as if seriousness requires pessimism. But the great leaps in human history were acts of deliberate hope—the decision to build democratic systems where none existed, to abolish entrenched injustices, to invest in public education, to develop medicines that eradicated diseases that we once took for granted as fate. None of those moves were realistic by the standards of their time. They became realistic because people chose to act as if they were.

The Intelligent Age asks for that same kind of courage. When intelligence becomes cheap and ubiquitous, what becomes scarce is meaning, unless we consciously cultivate it and design for it—unless we teach the next generation not only how to use AI, but how to imagine with it, argue with it, and dream beyond it. This is not a promise of utopia. It's a demand for responsibility.

The future worth wanting will not be defined by what AI can do. It will be defined by what we decide to do with AI. Do we use it to elevate dignity or to erode it? Do we use it to deepen connection or to distract from it? Do we use it to expand imagination or to narrow it to what is most profitable, clickable, or controllable? Do we raise children to be passive consumers of machine-generated reality or active stewards of meaning in a world of abundant intelligence? These are not technical questions. They are existential ones.

The real work of the Intelligent Age is not understanding how AI thinks, but taking responsibility for what we decide to do with that power.

And here, too, the mirror metaphor returns. AI reflects not just our intelligence but also our intentions. It shows us whether we care enough about the future to treat it as something we are responsible for, rather than something that simply happens to us. The crucial shift in mindset is this: The central question of the Intelligent Age is no longer "What will AI do to us?" The central question is "What will we choose to make possible because of AI?" Everything else flows from that.

A future worth wanting is not guaranteed. It has to be imagined, chosen, and built day by day, decision by decision, system by system. The technologies now at our disposal give us extraordinary leverage. They extend our reach, clarify our options, and accelerate the consequences of what we choose.

The real work of the Intelligent Age is not understanding how AI thinks, but taking responsibility for what we decide to do with that power.

The Next Human Is Not Post-Human

Every great turning point in human history has reshaped what it feels like to be human. Agriculture changed our bodies and rhythms. Industry changed our cities and daily routines. The Information Age changed our attention and our sense of time. The Intelligent Age does something more radical: It starts to change our identity.

AI doesn't just extend our abilities; it alters the psychological ground on which the self is built. For the first time, we're confronted with a form of intelligence that can mirror us, challenge us, amplify us, and sometimes surpass us. That encounter surfaces a question older than civilization but never as urgent as it is now: What does it mean to be human when intelligence is no longer ours alone? The question doesn't reduce us. It invites us. Because what made us human was never just our intelligence. It was our consciousness. It was our capacity for meaning, not just our capacity for calculation. It was our imagination, not just our efficiency.

The Intelligent Age reveals this by lifting some of the cognitive weight that once defined our worth. It gives us a glimpse, perhaps for the first time, of what humanity might look like when its mental architecture is no longer entirely shaped by survival, scarcity, and constraint.

As AI takes on more of the mechanics of thinking, humans gain access to something deeper: the experience of thinking. We begin to move from *performing* cognition to *directing* it. The mind stops functioning purely as a factory and begins to feel more like a studio.

When the external world becomes easier to manage cognitively, the internal world becomes cognitively richer. Reflection deepens. Awareness widens. Creativity intensifies. Curiosity, dulled by years of repetition and necessity, starts to wake up. Identity becomes less reactive and more intentional.

When people offload repetitive tasks and administrative clutter to machines, they start asking questions that once felt like luxuries reserved for late nights or midlife crises:

Who do I actually want to become?

What does a good life look like for me?

What genuinely brings me alive?

What have I been ignoring because there was "no time"?

What am I carrying that no longer belongs to me?

What dreams did I postpone because the world never made room for them?

AI can't answer those questions. But it can create the mental and emotional space in which we finally allow ourselves to ask them.

For most of history, creativity was framed as a privilege, something reserved for artists, composers, writers, and the occasional eccentric who could afford to devote time to the act of creation. The rest of the world was busy surviving—working for a living.

The Intelligent Age quietly upends that arrangement. When intelligence becomes a collaborator instead of a barrier, the palette of creativity is handed to everyone. You don't need to be a technical expert to design, compose, build, or explore. You need intent and curiosity. The system can handle much of the craft; you bring the direction.

Creativity stops being the product of isolated genius and becomes the outcome of relational imagination, a conversation between human intention and machine possibility. That doesn't flatten human originality. It amplifies it. It lets people venture into modes of expression that once felt too technical, too time-consuming, or too inaccessible to even attempt.

We move from seeing ourselves merely as "consumers" or occasional "creators" to seeing ourselves as conductors of creativity, orchestrating symphonies of image, text, sound, and experience in partnership with systems that expand what's possible.

When intelligence becomes a collaborator instead of a barrier, the palette of creativity is handed to everyone.

The "next human" is not defined by being smarter. The next human is defined by being deeper. Depth becomes the new frontier precisely because raw intelligence becomes abundant. You no longer prove your worth through effort alone or by hoarding expertise. Instead, you're invited, sometimes uncomfortably, to discover your worth through presence, clarity, and meaning.

The next human is the person who notices the thing the machine cannot—a mood, a meaning, a moment—and acts from that deeper layer of awareness. Imagine a doctor's office in the near future, an AI system will review a patient's scans, cross-reference twenty million cases, and produce a diagnosis with higher accuracy than any human radiologist.

But the patient doesn't ask the AI, "Does this mean I'm going to be okay?" They ask the doctor.

The next human is the doctor who sits down, breathes, looks the patient in the eyes, and says, "Let's talk about what this means for your life, not just your chart." Reassurance, interpretation, and shared humanity become the irreplaceable skill—not the identification of shadows on an image.

The real competition is no longer purely external; it is internal. Can you stay grounded while the world accelerates? Can you stay curious while so much is automated? Can you stay compassionate while polarization is algorithmically convenient? Can you stay unmistakably human while the definition of intelligence is being rewritten around you? That is the new psychological frontier.

AI also drags a deeper question into the spotlight, one we've mostly kept in the background: What is consciousness? When a machine appears to reason, reflect, or create, it forces us to examine the source of those same capacities in ourselves. For centuries, we've blurred the line between intelligence and consciousness, treating them almost as synonyms. The Intelligent Age exposes how wrong that was. Of all the things AI will force us to reimagine and better understand, human consciousness may be the single most important. We ask whether AI is conscious. What we most need to answer is what it means for us to be conscious.

Consciousness is not a byproduct of computation. It is the interiority of experience, the breath before the idea, the silence beneath the thought, the longing behind the choice, the meaning that supports purpose. AI doesn't touch this. It can simulate expression, but it cannot *experience* anything. It does not suffer, rejoice, hope, grieve, or love. It does not feel the weight of a decision or the ache of regret.

The next human is the human who finally understands this, not in an abstract philosophical way, but as an operating reality. Intelligence was never the pinnacle of our identity. Meaning was. And in the Intelligent Age, meaning doesn't disappear. It becomes the essence of what remains distinctly, irreducibly human.

The Intelligent Age is not an escape hatch from humanity. It is, in many ways, a return to it. The next human is not some engineered, post-biological being hovering above ordinary life. The next human is simply a person whose cognition is supported by AI, whose creativity is amplified by AI, whose choices are expanded by AI, and whose inner life deepens because of AI.

The next human is not owned by the machine. The next human is freed by it to explore identity, purpose, connection, and contribution at a scale and depth that so few in previous generations could afford; freed from the mental drudgery that kept so many asleep to their own potential; freed, ironically, to become more, not less, conscious.

AI does not complete the human story by replacing us. It completes the story by forcing us to finally inhabit what we are.

The Great Reconciliation

For as long as we've imagined the future, we've pictured a battlefield: human versus machine, creator versus creation. We've spun stories of overthrow and domination, of humans outsmarted or outmuscled by the very systems we built. Beneath all of them ran the same quiet fear—that if machines ever grew too capable, they would take something irreplaceable from us.

You can see that fear clearly in Fritz Lang's 1927 silent film *Metropolis,* where a gleaming machine-city is powered by an invisible underclass and a robotic double—the "machine-human"—is built to impersonate and ultimately replace a real woman. The machine doesn't just threaten to take human jobs; it threatens to take human identity, to mimic our image so perfectly that it can hijack our influence. Nearly a century before today's AI debates, *Metropolis* was already warning that the real terror isn't metal fists or laser eyes, but a machine that becomes convincing enough to stand in for us.

But the Intelligent Age doesn't play out like a showdown. It unfolds like a reconciliation, not with our machines, but with ourselves. From the earliest pages of this book, I've described AI as a mirror—reflective, confronting, and occasionally unforgiving. But here, at the end of this journey, the mirror shifts. It is no longer simply something we look into. It becomes something that hands us back pieces of ourselves we forgot were missing.

AI does not return a perfect likeness. It returns a deeper truth: that the essential parts of being human were never tied to the things machines are best at. What we feared was never the machine's intelligence. What we truly feared was the possibility that intelligence—as we defined it—might not be the core of our identity after all. We feared that if a machine could calculate faster, analyze better, or recall more, then maybe our value had been an illusion.

AI relentlessly, and gently, dismantles that illusion. It shows that our worth was never anchored in output. Productivity was never our purpose. Efficiency was never our essence. Our depth didn't come from what we *did* but from what we *felt, imagined, loved,* and *meant.* The reconciliation begins the moment we recognize this.

AI does more than reflect our contradictions and biases back to us. It also illuminates the space between who we are and who we could become. It exposes the creativity we pushed aside, the empathy we told ourselves we'd tend to "later," the purpose we kept postponing, and the courage we forgot we had. It highlights the habits we inherited and the potential we avoided. This is not a reconciliation between humans and machines. It is a reconciliation between the humans we have been and the fuller versions of ourselves we can become.

We've spent centuries thinking intelligence was a scarce resource—that if machines gained it, we would lose it. But intelligence doesn't behave like that. It scales. It multiplies. It opens new doors rather than closing the ones behind us.

Machine intelligence doesn't shrink human intelligence. It unburdens it. It releases us from the cognitive grind that chained our attention and creativity to survival, routine, and scarcity. What remains is the part of us that has always mattered most: the human capacity to find meaning in a world of endless possibility.

AI does more than reflect our contradictions and biases back to us. It also illuminates the space between who we are and who we could become.

AI doesn't replace humanity. It removes the weights we mistook for identity. The future will not pit humans against machines as competing species. It will weave both into an ecosystem—each doing what it does best. AI extends cognition outward into a global, tireless network. Humanity remains the center of consciousness, interpretation, intention, and moral choice. We do not fuse with the machinery. We orchestrate it. We become less like the workers and more like the conductors of our own cognitive symphony.

AI takes on the mechanical tasks of the mind so we can reclaim what has always been the real miracle of being human: reflection, imagination, empathy, creativity, connection, meaning—qualities no machine can counterfeit. Every major technological leap has given humanity a new tool. This leap gives us something unprecedented: a new possibility for ourselves.

The next era is not post-human or transhuman. It is fully human. It's humanity without the artificial limits that scarcity once imposed. A humanity that can spend its time on things that matter, a humanity capable of global insight rather than local reaction, a humanity guided by wisdom rather than fear, meaning rather than survival, and possibility rather than constraint.

> **We become less like the workers and more like the conductors of our own cognitive symphony.**

AI doesn't complete the human story by overpowering it. It completes the story by revealing the chapters we've left unwritten. In the end, the story of AI is not about machines learning to think. It's the story of humans learning to see clearly. It's the stark realization that what has always set us apart was never the engine of our logic, but the messy, beautiful, and unbreakable chaos of our consciousness. It's the part of us that feels before it thinks, that hopes when it should despair, that loves without reason, that creates without instruction, that chooses a future not because it is probable but because it is beautiful.

This is the mirror AI holds up. It does not diminish our humanity, nor does it define it for us. It simply reflects what we bring to it, our assumptions, our priorities, and our intentions, without comfort or disguise.

What unsettles us is not the machine itself, but the clarity it introduces. A clarity that makes it harder to hide behind necessity, tradition, or inertia. A clarity that reveals how often our limits were self-imposed, how much of what we accepted as fixed was simply unexamined.

The mirror does not tell us who to be. It shows us who we are becoming through the choices we make and the systems we build. And once that reflection is visible, it cannot be unseen.

That is the opportunity of the Intelligent Age. Not the end of the human story, and not its replacement, but a moment of reckoning. A chance to decide, with fewer illusions than ever before, what kind of people we intend to be, and what kind of civilization we are willing to take responsibility for creating.

The story of humanity is not ending.

We're just updating its byline.

Endnotes

Chapter 1

1 "Advaita Vedānta," Internet Encyclopedia of Philosophy, accessed January 3, 2026, https://iep.utm.edu/advaita-vedanta/.

2 Bhartrhari, Vākyapadīya. Bhartrhari argued that cognition is inseparable from language (śabda), denying the existence of fully formed, language-free thought. A parallel view appears in Ludwig Wittgenstein's *Philosophical Investigations,* where meaning is treated as inseparable from use.

3 Structural accounts of linguistic competence explain why systems can appear to reason without understanding. While Noam Chomsky distinguishes linguistic competence from performance, the present argument extends this distinction to deny that linguistic mastery alone entails cognition.

4 Bhartrhari's doctrine of *sphota* describes meaning as a holistic, instantaneous apprehension rather than a compositional assembly. Similar ideas appear in phenomenology; see Maurice Merleau-Ponty's *Phenomenology of Perception.*

5 This distinction echoes John Searle's "Chinese Room" argument, which demonstrates that symbol manipulation alone does not constitute understanding.

6 The warning against conflating representation with reality runs from Plato's allegory of the cave through modern critiques of technological rationality.

7 Joy Buolamwini and Timnit Gebru, "Gender Shades: Intersectional Accuracy Disparities in Commercial Gender Classification," *Proceedings of the Conference on Fairness, Accountability, and Transparency* (FAT, 2018): 77–91; see also research and advocacy by the Algorithmic Justice League.

8 Jeffrey Dastin, "Amazon Scraps Secret AI Recruiting Tool That Showed Bias Against Women," *Reuters,* October 10, 2018; see also Solon Barocas and Andrew D. Selbst, "Big Data's Disparate Impact," *California Law Review*

104, no. 3 (2016): 671–732. These studies document how hiring algorithms inherit and reinforce bias when trained on historical employment data shaped by discriminatory human decisions.

9 Organisation for Economic Co-operation and Development (OECD), *Using Artificial Intelligence to Help Combat COVID-19*, OECD Policy Responses to Coronavirus (Paris: OECD Publishing, 2020); and research initiatives associated with Google's SEED program, which applies large-scale social simulation and agent-based modeling to study misinformation spread, behavioral contagion, and collective response to economic and policy shocks. These models simulate human social dynamics rather than autonomous machine behavior.

10 John Nosta, "How AI Learned to Sound Like Thinking," *Psychology Today*, December 17, 2025, https://www.psychologytoday.com/us/blog/the-digital-self/202512/how-ai-learned-to-sound-like-thinking.

11 Barbara Starfield, Leiyu Shi, and James Macinko, "Contribution of Primary Care to Health Systems and Health," *Milbank Quarterly* 83, no. 3 (2005): 457–502; see also World Health Organization, *Primary Health Care: Now More Than Ever* (Geneva: WHO Press, 2008). Multiple studies cited in this literature show that strong primary care coordination is associated with reductions in total healthcare costs on the order of 20 percent to 30 percent, particularly through reduced hospitalizations, unnecessary specialist referrals, and duplicative testing.

12 Kathleen Fitzpatrick, Alison Darcy, and Molly Vierhile, "Delivering Cognitive Behavior Therapy to Young Adults with Symptoms of Depression and Anxiety Using a Fully Automated Conversational Agent (Woebot): A Randomized Controlled Trial," *JMIR Mental Health* 4, no. 2 (2017): e19. The study found that participants reported greater openness and reduced stigma when interacting with an AI-based CBT system, contributing to measurable improvements in mental health outcomes.

13 Shai Danziger, Jonathan Levav, and Liora Avnaim-Pesso, "Extraneous Factors in Judicial Decisions," *Proceedings of the National Academy of Sciences* 108, no. 17 (2011): 6889–6892. This widely cited study of Israeli parole boards demonstrated that favorable rulings declined sharply as judges became fatigued, with decisions resetting after food or rest breaks—evidence that cognitive depletion measurably influences judicial outcomes.

14 Daniel Kahneman, Olivier Sibony, and Cass R. Sunstein, *Noise: A Flaw in Human Judgment* (New York: Little, Brown Spark, 2021). Building on decades of behavioral research, the authors show that professional judgments—including legal decisions—are systematically shaped by situational factors and internal states that decision-makers themselves cannot reliably explain.

15 Stuart Russell, *Human Compatible: Artificial Intelligence and the Problem of Control* (New York: Viking, 2019), especially Chapter 2; see also Richard S. Sutton, "The Bitter Lesson," *Incomplete Ideas*, March 13, 2019, http://www.

incompleteideas.net/IncIdeas/BitterLesson.html. This body of research and analysis shows that AI systems—particularly reinforcement-learning and agent-based models—often achieve more reliable and empirically robust outcomes when optimized around broad objectives or reward functions, rather than narrowly specified rules or constraints that can lead to brittle behavior and unintended consequences.

Chapter 2

1 Nick Bostrom, "Ethical Issues in Advanced Artificial Intelligence," in *Cognitive, Emotive and Ethical Aspects of Decision Making in Humans and in Artificial Intelligence*, eds. Wendell Wallach, Iva Smit, G. E. Lasker (Windsor, ON: International Institute of Advanced Studies in Systems Research and Cybernetics, 2003): 12–17.

2 "Manhattan Project," Wikipedia, last modified January 2026, https://en.wikipedia.org/wiki/Manhattan_Project.

3 Thomas Moynihan, "The Fear of a Nuclear Fire That Would Consume Earth," BBC Future, September 8, 2023, https://www.bbc.com/future/article/20230907-the-fear-of-a-nuclear-fire-that-would-consume-earth.

4 Arnold Toynbee, *Lectures on the Industrial Revolution in England: Popular Addresses, Notes and Other Fragments*, ed. Benjamin Jowett (London: Rivingtons, 1884).

5 "AI in the Medical Field: 5 Examples Demonstrating its Efficacy," Aidoc, accessed January 3, 2026, https://www.aidoc.com/learn/blog/ai-in-the-medical-field-5-examples/.

6 Arthur C. Clarke and Stephen Baxter, The Light of Other Days (New York: Tor Books, 2000).

7 Werner Mostert, Anish Kurien, and Karim Djouani, "Multi-Modal Emotion Detection and Tracking System Using AI Techniques," *Computers* 14, no. 10 (October 2025): 441, https://doi.org/10.3390/computers14100441; Andrew McStay, "Emotional AI, Soft Biometrics and the Surveillance of Emotional Life: An Unusual Consensus on Privacy," *Big Data & Society* 7, no. 1 (March 2020), https://doi.org/10.1177/2053951720904386.

Chapter 3

1 Karl Popper, "Of Clouds and Clocks: An Approach to the Problem of Rationality and the Freedom of Man," in *Objective Knowledge: An Evolutionary Approach* (Oxford: Clarendon Press, 1972): 206–255.

2 European Union Aviation Safety Agency, *EASA Artificial Intelligence Roadmap 2.0: A Human-Centric Approach to AI in Aviation* (Cologne, Germany: EASA, May 2023), https://www.easa.europa.eu/en/domains/research-innovation/ai.

3 Plato, *The Republic*, trans. Benjamin Jowett, Book VII, 514a–520a.

4 John Pavlus, "'World Models,' an Old Idea in AI, Mount a Comeback," *Quanta Magazine*, September 2, 2025, https://www.quantamagazine.org/world-models-an-old-idea-in-ai-mount-a-comeback-20250902/.

5 Fei-Fei Li, "From Words to Worlds: Spatial Intelligence is AI's Next Frontier," Dr. Fei-Fei Li (Substack), November 10, 2025, https://drfeifei.substack.com/p/from-words-to-worlds-spatial-intelligence.

6 Ibid.

7 Lakshmi Varanasi, "6 Leading Humanoid Robot Companies Worth Watching," *Business Insider*, November 27, 2025, https://www.businessinsider.com/humanoid-robot-companies-us-tesla-figure-1x-agility-apptronik-2025-11.

8 Joseph Mapue, "21 Top Companies in the Vanguard of the Rise of Humanoid Robots," Ross Dawson, July 14, 2025, https://rossdawson.com/futurist/companies-creating-future/top-companies-rise-humanoid-robots/.

9 James Somers, "A Revolution in How Robots Learn," *The New Yorker*, November 25, 2024, https://www.newyorker.com/magazine/2024/12/02/a-revolution-in-how-robots-learn.

10 Jack Monas and Eric Jang, "1X World Model," 1X Discover, September 17, 2024, https://www.1x.tech/discover/1x-world-model.

11 Yann LeCun, "A Path Towards Autonomous Machine Intelligence," June 27, 2022, https://openreview.net/pdf?id=BZ5a1r-kVsf.

12 Iason Gabriel, "Artificial Intelligence, Values, and Alignment," *Minds and Machines* 30, no. 3 (October 2020): 411–437, https://doi.org/10.1007/s11023-020-09539-2.

13 Harry S. Truman Presidential Library & Museum, "Decision to Drop the Atomic Bomb," accessed January 3, 2026, https://www.trumanlibrary.gov/education/presidential-inquiries/decision-drop-atomic-bomb. It should be noted that there has been considerable debate as to whether Truman's decision was influenced by the lives that might be saved or his concern that, without the USA's use of an atomic bomb, Russia might invade Japan, resulting in territorial concerns after Japan's eventual surrender.

14 Kaitlyn Gomez, "The Conscience Hacker: How One Visionary Is Rewiring AI to Care," *Rolling Stone UK*, October 8, 2025, https://www.rollingstone.co.uk/culture/the-conscience-hacker-how-one-visionary-is-rewiring-ai-to-care-54653/.

Chapter 4

1 Oscar Gelderblom, Abe de Jong, and Joost Jonker, "The Formative Years of the Modern Corporation: The Dutch East India Company VOC, 1602–1623," *The Journal of Economic History* 73, no. 4 (December 2013): 1050–1076, https://doi.org/10.1017/S0022050713000879.

2 Ibid.

3 More precisely, corporate personhood existed in rare, exceptional cases during this period—most notably the English East India Company (founded 1600) and the Dutch VOC (founded 1602), which were granted special royal charters with legal personhood, permanent capital, and limited liability. However, these were extraordinary monopolies, not the general rule. Most businesses in the seventeenth and eighteenth centuries operated as partnerships or sole proprietorships, where responsibility flowed directly to individual owners. Corporate personhood did not become widely accessible until the nineteenth century, particularly after the Santa Clara County decision in 1886. See Gelderblom, de Jong, and Jonker, 2013.

4 The US Copyright Office has clarified that purely AI-generated works are not copyrightable absent meaningful human authorship, and courts have upheld this requirement, reinforcing that ownership hinges on human creative contribution rather than mechanical generation. (US Copyright Office, *Copyright and AI*, 2025; Reuters coverage of federal appeals court decision).

5 US Securities and Exchange Commission, "SEC Charges Knight Capital With Violations of Market Access Rule," Press Release 2013–222, October 16, 2013, https://www.sec.gov/newsroom/press-releases/2013-222.

6 John Jumper et al., "Highly Accurate Protein Structure Prediction with AlphaFold," *Nature* 596, no. 7873 (July 15, 2021): 583–589, https://doi.org/10.1038/s41586-021-03819-2.

7 Irene B. Meier et al., "Using a Digital Neuro Signature to Measure Longitudinal Individual-Level Change in Alzheimer's Disease: The Altoida Large Cohort Study," *npj Digital Medicine* 4, no. 101 (June 24, 2021), https://doi.org/10.1038/s41746-021-00470-z.

8 International Energy Agency, "Energy and AI: Energy Demand from AI," IEA, 2024, https://www.iea.org/reports/energy-and-ai/energy-demand-from-ai.

9 Friedrich Nietzsche, *Thus Spoke Zarathustra: A Book for All and None*, trans. R. J. Hollingdale (1883–1885; London: Penguin Books, 1961), Prologue, section 5; Friedrich Nietzsche, *Beyond Good and Evil: Prelude to a Philosophy of the Future*, trans. Walter Kaufmann (1886; New York: Vintage Books, 1966), sections 199–203.

Chapter 5

1 Strada Education Foundation and Burning Glass Institute, "Talent Disrupted: College Graduates, Underemployment, and the Way Forward," February 2024; Sara Weissman, "More Than Half of Recent 4-Year College Grads Underemployed," *Inside Higher Ed*, February 22, 2024, https://www.insidehighered.com/news/students/academics/2024/02/22/more-half-recent-four-year-college-grads-underemployed.

2 Erik Brynjolfsson, Bharat Chandar, and Ruyu Chen, "Canaries in the Coal Mine? Six Facts about the Recent Employment Effects of Artificial

Intelligence," Stanford Digital Economy Lab working paper, August 26, 2025; Trevor Laurence Jockims, "AI Isn't Just Ending Entry-Level Jobs. It's the End of the Career Ladder as We Know It," *CNBC*, September 7, 2025, https://www.cnbc.com/2025/09/07/ai-entry-level-jobs-hiring-careers.html.

3 "How Pieter Levels Built a $3M/Year Business with Zero Employees," Fast-SaaS, October 29, 2025, https://www.fast-saas.com/blog/pieter-levels-success-story/.

4 Justin Welsh, *The One-Person Business*, Substack, https://www.justinwelsh.me; see also Justin Welsh, LinkedIn posts and interviews documenting his use of AI-enabled content workflows to analyze trends, generate content, and engage audiences at scale, 2022–2024.

Chapter 6

1 Michael R. Siebecker, "A New Corporate Governance Paradigm for the AI Revolution," The CLS Blue Sky Blog, January 17, 2025, https://clsbluesky.law.columbia.edu/2025/01/17/a-new-corporate-governance-paradigm-for-the-ai-revolution/.

2 Jake Yu, "Building Trust in AI Through a New Global Governance Framework," World Economic Forum, November 10, 2025, https://www.weforum.org/stories/2025/11/trust-ai-global-governance/.

3 Jake Yu, "Building Trust in AI Through a New Global Governance Framework," World Economic Forum, November 10, 2025, https://www.weforum.org/stories/2025/11/trust-ai-global-governance/.

4 Malihe Alikhani and Sabit Hassan, "Hype and Harm: Why We Must Ask Harder Questions About AI and Its Alignment with Human Values," Brookings Institution, October 9, 2025, https://www.brookings.edu/articles/hype-and-harm-why-we-must-ask-harder-questions-about-ai-and-its-alignment-with-human-values/.

5 Hayden Field, "OpenAI Dissolves Team Focused on Long-term AI Risks, Less Than One Year After Announcing It," CNBC, May 17, 2024, https://www.cnbc.com/2024/05/17/openai-superalignment-sutskever-leike.html.

6 UNESCO, "Recommendation on the Ethics of Artificial Intelligence," adopted November 23, 2021, https://www.unesco.org/en/artificial-intelligence/recommendation-ethics.

7 "Joint Statement From Founding Members of the Global Partnership on Artificial Intelligence," US Department of State, June 15, 2020, https://2021-2025.state.gov/joint-statement-from-founding-members-of-the-global-partnership-on-artificial-intelligence/.

8 Universal basic income trials in Kenya (GiveDirectly, "Early Findings from the World's Largest UBI Study," December 6, 2023, https://www.givedirectly.org/2023-ubi-results/), Finland (Ministry of Social Affairs and Health, Finland, "Results of the Basic Income Experiment," May 6,

2020, https://stm.fi/en/-/perustulokokeilun-tulokset-tyollisyysvaikutukset-vahaisia-toimeentulo-ja-psyykkinen-terveys-koettiin-paremmaksi), and several US cities, including Stockton, California (Rachel Treisman, "California Program Giving $500 No-Strings-Attached Stipends Pays Off, Study Finds," NPR, March 4, 2021, https://www.npr.org/2021/03/04/973653719/california-program-giving-500-no-strings-attached-stipends-pays-off-study-finds) have provided early data on guaranteed income programs.

9 Isaac Asimov, "Runaround," in *I, Robot* (New York: Doubleday, 1950), 40.

10 David Hambling, "Ukrainian AI Attack Drones May Be Killing without Human Oversight," *New Scientist*, October 13, 2023 Dan Sabbagh, "US Air Force Denies Running Simulation in Which AI Drone 'Killed' Operator," *The Guardian*, June 2, 2023, https://www.theguardian.com/us-news/2023/jun/01/us-military-drone-ai-killed-operator-simulated-test. Note: Col. Tucker Hamilton, the USAF's Chief of AI Test and Operations, subsequently stated that he "mis-spoke" and that the scenario was a hypothetical "thought experiment" rather than an actual simulation. The Air Force issued a formal denial, stating it had never conducted any such AI-drone simulation. See Royal Aeronautical Society, "Highlights from the RAeS Future Combat Air & Space Capabilities Summit," updated June 2, 2023. See also: Vincent Boulanin and Maaike Verbruggen, *Mapping the Development of Autonomy in Weapon Systems* (Stockholm International Peace Research Institute, November 2017); and Human Rights Watch, "Stopping Killer Robots: Country Positions on Banning Fully Autonomous Weapons and Retaining Human Control," August 2020.

11 James Vincent, "Satya Nadella's Rules for AI Are More Boring (and Relevant) Than Asimov's Three Laws," *The Verge*, June 29, 2016, https://www.theverge.com/2016/6/29/12057516/satya-nadella-ai-robot-laws.

12 James Vincent, "Google's AI Researchers Say These Are the Five Key Problems for Robot Safety," *The Verge*, June 22, 2016, https://www.theverge.com/circuitbreaker/2016/6/22/11999664/google-robots-ai-safety-five-problems.

13 European Parliament, "Regulation (EU) 2024/1689 of the European Parliament and of the Council of 13 June 2024 Laying Down Harmonized Rules on Artificial Intelligence (Artificial Intelligence Act)," *Official Journal of the European Union*, July 12, 2024; Seaton Huang, Helen Toner, Zac Haluza, and Rogier Creemers, "Translation: Measures for the Management of Generative Artificial Intelligence Services (Draft for Comment)," DigiChina, Stanford University, April 2023.

14 Republic of Estonia e-Residency Programme, "Estonian e-Residency Community Reaches 100,000 Members," Press Release, February 22, 2023, https://www.e-resident.gov.ee/blog/posts/estonian-e-residency-community-reaches-100000-members/.

15 International Telecommunication Union (ITU), "Facts and Figures 2023: Global Offline Population Steadily Declines to 2.6 Billion people in 2023," Press Release, September 12, 2023.

16 SkillsFuture Singapore, "Annual Report 2022–2023," https://www.skillsfuture.gov.sg/.

17 SkillsFuture Singapore (SSG), "SkillsFuture Year-in-Review 2024," SkillsFuture Singapore, 2025, https://www.ssg.gov.sg/newsroom/skillsfuture-year-in-review-2024/; SSG, "More Employers and Mid-Career Workers Taking Up SSG-Supported Training," SkillsFuture Singapore, 2024, https://www.ssg.gov.sg/newsroom/more-employers-and-mid-career-workers-taking-up-ssg-supported-training/. See also "SkillsFuture Credit," MySkillsFuture, https://www.myskillsfuture.gov.sg/content/portal/en/career-resources/career-resources/education-career-personal-development/SkillsFuture_Credit.html. On participation disparities by occupation, see Chan Chun Sing, "Future-Skilling the Workforce: SkillsFuture Movement in Singapore," in *International Handbook of Skill, Education, Training and the Transition to Work* (Springer, 2023).

18 Finnish National Agency for Education, "New National Core Curriculum for Basic Education: Focus on Phenomenon-Based Learning," 2016.

19 Ziad Obermeyer, Brian Powers, Christine Vogeli, Sendhil Mullainathan, "Dissecting Racial Bias in an Algorithm Used to Manage the Health of Populations," *Science* 366, no. 6464 (October 25, 2019): 447–453, https://www.science.org/doi/10.1126/science.aax2342. The study found the algorithm affected healthcare decisions for over 200 million people annually in the United States.

20 Joy Buolamwini and Timnit Gebru, "Gender Shades: Intersectional Accuracy Disparities in Commercial Gender Classification," *Proceedings of Machine Learning Research* 81 (2018): 1–15.

21 Rebecca Heilweil, "Big Tech Companies Back Away from Selling Facial Recognition to Police," *Vox*, June 11, 2020, https://www.vox.com/recode/2020/6/10/21287194/amazon-microsoft-ibm-facial-recognition-moratorium-police. IBM announced it would no longer offer general-purpose facial recognition software in June 2020, followed by similar announcements from Amazon and Microsoft.

22 Torben M. Andersen and Michael Svarer, "Flexicurity: Labour Market Performance in Denmark," *CESifo Economic Studies* 53, no. 3 (2007): 389–429.

23 OECD, "Economic Surveys: Denmark 2023," Organisation for Economic Co-operation and Development, 2023.

24 This example is illustrative based on general patterns in corporate automation transitions. Specific company case studies vary, and success rates depend heavily on program design, industry, and worker demographics. For broader context, see Daron Acemoglu and Pascual Restrepo, "Automation and New Tasks: How Technology Displaces and Reinstates Labor," *Journal of Economic Perspectives* 33, no. 2 (2019): 3–30.

25 Georgia Wells, Jeff Horwitz, and Deepa Seetharaman, "Facebook Knows Instagram Is Toxic for Teen Girls, Company Documents Show," *Wall Street Journal*, September 14, 2021 (discusses similar algorithmic optimization across social media platforms), https://www.wsj.com/tech/personal-tech/facebook-knows-instagram-is-toxic-for-teen-girls-company-documents-show-11631620739.

26 Sensor Tower, "Store Intelligence User Behavior Report," Q4 2023.

27 Internal ByteDance documents cited in Rob Barry, Georgia Wells, John West, Joanna Stern, and Jason French, "How TikTok Serves Up Sex and Drug Videos to Minors," *Wall Street Journal*, September 8, 2021, https://www.wsj.com/tech/tiktok-algorithm-sex-drugs-minors-11631052944.

28 Jonathan Haidt, "The Dangerous Experiment on Teen Girls," *The Atlantic*, November 21, 2021, https://www.theatlantic.com/ideas/archive/2021/11/facebooks-dangerous-experiment-teen-girls/620767/; see also Jonathan Haidt, Jean Twenge, and Zach Rausch, *Social Media and Mental Health: A Collaborative Review*, unpublished manuscript, New York University. Accessed at tinyurl.com/SocialMediaMentalHealthReview.

29 OpenAI, "GPT-4 System Card," March 2023, 59–68, https://cdn.openai.com/papers/gpt-4-system-card.pdf

30 Colin Lecher, "What Happens When an Algorithm Cuts Your Healthcare," *The Verge*, March 21, 2018; Legal Aid of Arkansas litigation documents in *Arkansas Department of Human Services v. Ledgerwood* and related cases.

31 District Court of The Hague, *NJCM c.s. v. De Staat der Nederlanden (SyRI case)*, Case No. C/09/550982 / HA ZA 18-388, Judgment of February 5, 2020. The court found the SyRI system violated Article 8 of the European Convention on Human Rights (right to respect for private and family life).

32 Thomas Koulopoulos, *Revealing the Invisible: How Our Hidden Behaviors Are Becoming the Most Valuable Commodity of the 21st Century* (Tennessee, USA: Post Hill Press, 2018).

Acknowledgments

Despite the tremendous din that surrounds the topic of AI, writing about a hopeful future can, at times, feel rather lonely. We have been inundated with the classic Hollywood trope of AI cast as the last great human invention, a competitor, and an existential threat to humanity. These are themes that have echoed throughout history as new technologies have threatened to displace humans. The difference this time is the speed of the change. Which is why, now more than ever, it has been essential for me to rely on a network of friends and colleagues to help ground, shape, and align my view of the future.

It seems folly to try and list all those who've influenced my thinking. Far too many conversations went into shaping *The Mirror.* However, there are some people who've been significant in helping me to look critically at AI and its impact. Acknowledging them is as much a statement of respect for their thinking as it is an admission of my own need for clarity in the midst of accelerating complexity.

Sunil Malhotra, author of YOGAi, has long had a deep influence on my understanding of not only AI but the deeper issues that shape our thinking and our behaviors. His decidedly non-Western view of the world has provided a critical balance and clarity to how AI will elevate the very human task of seeing ourselves and our purpose more clearly. Sunil reminds me often of how important it is to open our minds to ways of thinking that expand our understanding of the world. His calm and measured tenor never fails to help me see with greater clarity.

Jim Hayes, Principle at Aspire Group, has also been a long-time collaborator. A polymath and a deep thinker with a broad understanding of the human condition, his insights have often led me down paths that have become cornerstones of my thinking and guideposts to help me frame the transitions we are going through. Jim introduced me to the work of Sir Karl Popper, whose thinking has become one of the central themes in much of my writing and thinking over the past decade. More importantly, he has taught me, through example, to embrace uncertainty and challenge as an opportunity to rise and thrive.

One of the first people to read and comment on an early draft of The Mirror was Ernie Carabillo, CEO of Humintel. Ernie is one of those rare individuals who has the gift of creating extraordinary teams and that turn vision into reality. His work in enabling many of the concepts that I have long written about gives me hope in the value of using AI to elevate human dignity in practical ways that will benefit all humanity. While I may pontificate on the future, Ernie is busy building it.

One of the most demanding aspects of writing is bringing in fresh ideas. In the case of AI, the field is moving so fast that the energy needed to keep up can often feel overwhelming. My answer to this has always been to surround myself with friends and colleagues who are much younger and smarter, and whose vision of the future is not shackled by their past. Vlas Vlastos is one of those rare individuals. Vlas has brought immense energy, incredible vision, and deep insight to stretch my understanding of what AI is capable of and to remind me of the value of boundless enthusiasm unencumbered by the constraints of the past.

Jeetu Patel, President at Cisco, who was kind enough to write the foreword for The Mirror, is one of my oldest friends. I've had the privilege of watching his passion and brilliance take him on an incredible journey over the past three decades. His achievement and the respect he has earned are a testimonial to how success need not come at the cost of humility and caring. Jeetu is one of the pioneers leading the next generation of AI, and I, for one, am far more hopeful knowing that his hand and heart are helping to shape the future.

I also made the deliberate decision to walk the walk and use AI as an intimate collaborator in the writing of The Mirror. If I was to write about the power of AI in helping us to reevaluate ourselves, our ideas, and our values, then I had to hold the mirror up to myself. After writing fourteen books, I was more than a bit suspect of AI's ability to provide anything novel or remotely collaborative, much less to understand my voice and to amplify rather than suppress it.

Nevertheless, I built a small team of editorial agents to critique my thinking and my writing. I would often ask them to review what I had written and to ruthlessly deconstruct my arguments based on their merits and clarity. I'd take the critique of one agent and feed it to a second, and then a third agent, each one specialized in different aspects of writing, from copy editing and accuracy, to references and footnotes, to the consistency of narrative. As these agents became familiar with The Mirror, as well as my thinking, they evolved in ways I wasn't expecting. While I did not experience what I'd term novelty in their insights, the level of understanding they exhibited surprised me.

What I found in that process was my own experience of the mirror. As my ideas were reflected back to me, I was able to identify areas where I needed to rethink or reconsider my own perspectives. AI did not write for me, but it most definitely shaped both what and how I wrote. I had not anticipated the power of living so closely with my own thoughts being played back to me, critiqued in real time, and, ultimately, amplified in ways and in directions I might not have taken otherwise. My takeaway: the line between us and the machine has never been harder to distinguish.

Of all the people who have influenced my thinking and my personal evolution, my greatest blessing in keeping up with the future has been my children. Seeing the world through their eyes of opportunity and wonder has been my most invaluable education. I spend my life peering into the future to help others navigate it, but my own path forward is best illuminated by their candor, brilliance, and guidance. Mia and Adam, I admire your honesty and integrity, I am awestruck by your brilliance, I am grateful for how you challenge me, and I am proud of the courage you have to follow your dreams. For me, you are the best part of the future.

Lastly, I am most grateful to you, the reader. Authors write to be read, and without your interest, there is no purpose or meaning to writing. It's a humbling experience to hear from people who have read my books and, in some small way, have been influenced by my ideas and opinions. But the greatest joy is hearing from people who have found inspiration in my writing, which helped them develop their own interpretation and understanding of the future. That is perhaps the most human of all connections—the ability to inspire others to find their own meaning. It's in that magnificent and awkward intellectual dance between humans—where words spark innovation—that the future is born.

About the Author

Thomas Koulopoulos is chairman and founder of Delphi Group, a Boston-based think tank he has led for more than thirty-five years. He is also the founding partner of Acrovantage Ventures, investing in early-stage companies shaping the future of work, health care, and enterprise innovation.

An author of fifteen books, an inventor with multiple patents, and past executive director of the Babson Center for Business Innovation, Koulopoulos brings more than four decades of experience at the intersection of technology, business, and human behavior. He is best known for exploring how emerging technologies reshape leadership, values, and purpose. A globally sought-after keynote speaker, he is known for engaging, entertaining, and challenging audiences to rethink not just how they run their organizations but how they see their future.